The Christmas Match

PEHR THERMAENIUS

The Christmas Match

UNIFORM
PRESS

Uniform Press Ltd
66 Charlotte Street
London
W1T 4QE

www.uniformpress.co.uk

10 9 8 7 6 5 4 3 2

This edition published in 2014
First published in Sweden by Bokförlaget Atlantis AB 2014

Text copyright Pehr Thermaenius
Original cover design and maps copyright Patrik Sundström
English language design copyright Tora Kelly

ISBN 978-1-910500-01-9

Printed in the UK by Short Run Press.

Contents

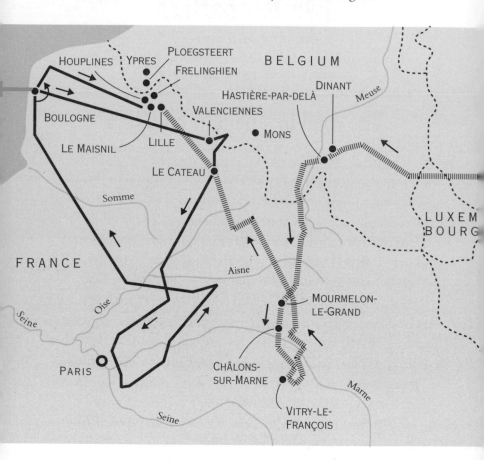

|||||||||| Albert Schmidt's unit. The Ninth Royal Saxon Infantry Regiment No. 133.
It was called IR133.

18 August: Into Belgium.
22 August: Hastière-par-delà.
4 September: Châlons-sur-Marne.
6-10 September: Vitry-le-François.
11 September: Back over the Marne.

Until 4 October: In trenches near
Mourmelon-le-Grand.
11 October: Near Lille.
The end of October to the end of the
year: Near Frelinghien

HOUPLINES YPRES PLOEGSTEERT
FRELINGHIEN
BELGIUM
HASTIÈRE-PAR-DELÀ DINANT Meuse
BOULOGNE VALENCIENNES
LE MAISNIL LILLE MONS
LE CATEAU
Somme
LUXEM
BOURG
FRANCE
Aisne
Oise
MOURMELON-
LE-GRAND
Seine
PARIS
CHÂLONS-
SUR-MARNE
Marne
VITRY-LE-
FRANÇOIS
Seine

—— Jimmy Coyle's unit. The Second Battalion, Argyll and Sutherland Highlanders. It was
called the 93rd.

11 August: To Boulogne.
22 August: Valenciennes.
24 August: Turned to the south.
26 August: Battle of Le Cateau.
6 September: Turned to the north near
Paris.

22 September–5 October: At the Aisne.
21 October: The fight at Le Maisnil.
9-13 November: The attack at Ploegsteert
Wood.
17 November to the end of the year: Near
Houplines.

Two footballers

The road to a field in Flanders

The war in Flanders between German and British soldiers fell silent on Christmas Eve 1914. The soldiers stopped shooting and started singing. On Christmas Day they came out of their trenches and met in No Man's Land. Some played football. This story is about two men, both footballers and soldiers, one Saxon and one Scot. They were in units that played a match in a field, between the French villages of Houplines and Frelinghien.

Albert Schmidt played inside right in the third team of Fussballclub 02 Schedewitz, a small town bordering the garrison town of Zwickau – in Saxony in eastern Germany. He was a conscript soldier and Gefreiter, the equivalent of lance corporal, in the 9th Saxon Regiment, which was number 133 in the German Army. Albert was awarded the Iron Cross, Second Class, for his conduct in a fight in 1914. He was killed on 20 August 1916. His grave is in the German war cemetery in the French village of Villers-au-Flos.

Sergeant James Coyle was a professional soldier in the 2nd Battalion of the Argyll and Sutherland Highlanders Regiment.

7

He was captain of the battalion football team and before the war he played a few games as inside left for Albion Rovers, a professional club in the second division of the Scottish league. When war broke out his battalion was based at Fort George, near Inverness in Scotland. James, who was most probably called Jimmy, survived the war. He was awarded the Military Medal for his conduct in a fight in 1918.

It is not possible to say for sure that Albert and Jimmy played each other or that they met during the Christmas Truce. Germany and Britain damaged each other's archives from the First World War when they bombed each other's cities during the Second World War. The war diaries of the 133rd Regiment and lists of soldiers are not to be found in Sächsisches Staatsarchiv in Dresden. The war diaries of the Argyll and Sutherland Highlanders are in The National Archives in London, but most documents with information about individual soldiers were lost. But fortunately there is much to be learnt about these two units in surviving diaries, letters and accounts of the war. With the help of these sources I have been able to follow Albert and Jimmy through the war to that hard, frozen field in Flanders that became a football pitch on Christmas Day.

Both Albert and Jimmy were in the war from its beginning, in August 1914, and both of them must have believed it would be a short war. The German Emperor told soldiers that they would be home before the leaves had fallen from the trees. British officers and politicians thought the war would be over by Christmas. But that did not happen. The time up to Christmas came to be less than one tenth of the duration of the war.

Albert Schmidt's regiment went into the war with just over

Sergeant James Coyle was a professional soldier in the second Battalion, Argyll and Sutherland Highlanders. He was also captain of the Battalion football team before and after the war. (Argyll and Sutherland Highlanders.)

3,300 men. By Christmas the regiment had reported at least 2,141 soldiers lost: killed, wounded, missing or taken prisoner. Also, many soldiers must have left the regiment because they were ill or injured in accidents that were not caused by the enemy. About 1,800 replacement soldiers had come to the regiment in the period before Christmas.

Jimmy Coyle's battalion landed in France with just over 1,000 men which was also the strength at Christmas. I have found reports of about 860 lost soldiers. But a more reliable measure of the casualties is probably the number of new soldiers who came to the battalion before Christmas: 1,134 men.

So at Christmas the German regiment had lost a number of soldiers roughly corresponding to two-thirds of the number that went into the war. The British battalion had lost more soldiers than came to France in August.

Therefore one should not look on the German regiment and the British battalion as two large groups of men who marched off and fought together during autumn and the beginning of the winter. Most of the soldiers who met between the trenches on Christmas Day did not take part in the first fighting in August. And most of those who were there in August were no longer there at Christmas.

But Albert and Jimmy were there. By Christmas they had learnt to live in muddy trenches, with lice and rats and the smell of bad latrines and decomposing human bodies. And there was also the risk of at any moment losing a friend or losing one's own life. But during an hour or so on Christmas Day these two forwards could forget the war. Other things became important, like an opening pass or, better, a good shot into the goal.

There is no picture of Lance Corporal Albert Schmidt. He was a conscripted soldier in the Ninth Royal Saxon Infantry Regiment, number 133. The picture shows other soldiers in the Regiment on his way to the war.
(Manfred Beyer)

Albert and Jimmy

The boys from Schedewitz

Fussballclub 02 Schedewitz lost 18 players when Germany mobilized on 2 August 1914. These players were members of the Club's three teams for the 1912–1913 season in the Western Saxony league. But the names of these 18 players do not appear in the line-ups for the 1914–1915 season. It is not probable that they lost their places in the teams because they were not good enough. The club's history, written for its 25th anniversary in 1927, says that the club lost so many players to the army that there were only enough players left for one team. If any of the 18 players had been free to play there would surely have been a place for them in a team.

The city of Zwickau, of which Schedewitz was a working-class suburb, had 75,000 inhabitants in 1912. It was a centre for industry, trade, education, culture and administration in Saxony. Zwickau was also a military town. Its most prestigious regiment was the Ninth Royal Saxon Infantry Regiment No. 133. It was usually called IR133.

The coal mines dominated the Zwickau economy. A

panorama of the coal fields drawn in 1857, shows 39 chimneys, and 28 mines are listed in the caption. Later in the century more and deeper mines were built. The owners of the mines, at first called coal farmers, formed large corporations and became coal barons.

It was thanks to the coal mines that Zwickau and its suburbs developed into an industrial area. Coal was first used in steam engines that powered water pumps. Later the entire machinery of the mines was powered by steam and coal, and when production grew, coal was also needed for the engines that brought the coal to customers in southern Germany. The coal industry drove the development of the railways. Each pit had its own track. Zwickau was one of Germany's most important freight rail hubs.

Enterprises moved to Zwickau to be near the coal. The mines also drove technical development. The Zwickau Mining School opened in 1862 and the Technical College opened in 1897 with education in machinery and electrical engineering. The technical development made it possible to start other enterprises.

First came companies that had a direct connection with mining, such as manufacturers of railway equipment and the world's leading manufacturer of mining lamps, Friemann & Wolf. This company was based on a new invention, a safety lamp that burned paraffin. Before that, miners used rape oil lamps that gave less light and caused methane explosions. In the years before the war Friemann & Wolf developed the first electrical, battery-powered, headlamp. By then 900 people worked in the company and it had subsidiaries around the world.

Then came companies that had no direct link with the mines, but were attracted by the big corporations in the coal

Coal mining drove industry around Zwickau and Schedewitz. This
picture shows the Oberhohndorf Forst pit around 1900.
(Norbert Peschke)

industry and the technological development. Among those were
companies in the textile industry, a porcelain china factory and car
manufacturers. August Horch and a group of partners built a car
factory in 1904. Then, a few years later, Horch left the company
after a disagreement with his partners. He built a new car plant,

which competed for customers with the first factory and he also named his new company after himself. But a court decided that this name belonged to his former partners. Horch then changed the name. He called his company Audi, which comes from the Latin word for "listen!", which is "horch!" in German.

The growth of the mines changed Schedewitz. Before coal began to be mined in the area around the middle of the 19th century the village had a few hundred inhabitants. Around the turn of the century the population had grown to about 6,000. Those who lived there worked in the mines and in the industries around the mines. The Social Democrats, the unions and the cooperative movement were strong. The Cooperative Society of Schedewitz was one of the first in Germany and when the cooperative societies in Germany formed a trading company the largest capital contribution came from the Schedewitz Society.

Those who lived in Schedewitz prospered during the years up to the war in the sense that they had jobs but the smoke that came out of the chimneys was ugly and it polluted the air. Some jobs were unhealthy or downright dangerous. A miner who was invalided for life received a pension that was a third of what his wife earned as a factory worker. The mines also affected Schedewitz visibly, making the ground sink several metres. Houses leaned and their walls cracked. Pipes for water and sewage burst when the land sank, so many homes were substandard and unhealthy. The diseases of the time had Schedewitz in a firm grip. But the town was also favoured by the technical development. There was a tram line from Schedewitz to the railway station in Zwickau. The price of a ticket was about the same as the price for a litre of milk.

A high school student is said to have brought the first football to Zwickau. He had been to England from where he also brought a referee's whistle. High school students are known to have played football in 1885, at the time when many of the men who later went into the war were born. The high school students played on common land in the city. Football became popular. Boys who lived along a street formed a team and played boys from other streets. But there was no football club until just before the turn of the century when the tennis club at the Technical College took up football.

Football in Germany had started as an upper class sport with diplomats among the first players. But soon football spread to the working class. Twelve boys in Schedewitz formed a club in 1902, Fussballclub 02 Schedewitz. Formalities probably were at a minimum. No documents and just a few match results from the first years have survived. The boys started to practise on a playing field and in the spring of 1904 they felt ready to challenge the Technical College students. And the boys won 2–1. That meant the club was established and the members pooled their money to buy a match outfit: blue shorts, white shirts and real football boots.

The club's young founding members understood that they must recruit new members and train them to become players. Kicking about was no longer good enough. Recruiting cannot have been difficult. Football grew rapidly in Saxony and the game received a boost in 1903 when the Leipzig team won the final of the first German championship. At this time those who would become soldiers in the war were teenagers and eager to take up the new game. So the club grew and moved to a new field by the river Mulde. It was far from ideal and the members had to work hard to make it playable, but it was better than the original playing ground.

The club fielded two teams who played other clubs in and around Zwickau with mixed results. In the summer of 1911 the club put up a third team. Football in the region was being organized and F. C. 02 Schedewitz' first team was given a place in the second division of the Western Saxony League. The team had a brilliant season, winning eleven games with two draws. The goal difference was an impressing, 55–11, and the team was promoted to the first division. The second team won all its matches and won its division. No results for the third team have survived.

When the club's first team started the 1913–1914 season, the players learnt what defeat feels like. But the team was strong enough to attract a good crowd, so the club could start charging gate money.

When Germany mobilized in the summer of 1914 and conscripted men were called to their regiments, it put a halt to the football club's encouraging development. The club took on new, young players to fill the gaps left by those who went into the army and there were two teams at the start of the season. But more and more players were called up and at the end of the season there were enough players for just one team.

The club history described what had happened:

"On the memorable day 1 August also the football club had to let some of its most reliable members go off to take part in the great struggle between the peoples, thereby giving up the sport that had become a necessity of life."

◉ JIMMY ◉

A vanman in Edinburgh

Jimmy Coyle signed as a professional soldier for the Argyll and Sutherland Highlanders on 6 March 1905. The regimental records tell us he was an eighteen-year-old vanman, or waggoner, born in St Giles' parish, Edinburgh. He was given the regimental number 9696.

Jimmy is the only soldier mentioned as a footballer who with certainty was a member of the battalion that played football against the Germans on Christmas Day. That is why he is one of the two main characters in this story.

From what I have been able to find out about him he was a talented, aspiring working-class boy. It seems he joined the army because he wanted something more than staying where he was, in the Irish community in Edinburgh's Old Town. The army promised to let him see something of the world, to give him education and a regular income. Perhaps he also liked the uniform. Girls were said to fancy kilted soldiers.

The name Coyle has an Irish ring to it. People from Ireland had migrated to Scotland for hundreds of years and the exodus grew in the middle of the 19th century when Ireland was struck by famine. Most Irish people settled on the west coast, mainly in Glasgow, but many also came to Edinburgh.

When the Irish came to Scotland they found themselves at the bottom of society. The immigrants had to content themselves with the worst places to live, like in some areas of the Old Town of Edinburgh. The Old Town was near the Castle and Holyrood

Palace, which is the official home in Scotland for the monarch of the United Kingdom. The rich and powerful had left the Old Town and had moved to the New Town, north of the valley that is now Princes Street Gardens. As the years passed and as more and more Irish immigrants came to Edinburgh, parts of the Old Town turned into a densely populated, isolated "Little Ireland". It was drenched in alcohol, it was a no go area for the police and it was regarded as one of Europe's worst slums.

When Jimmy Coyle was born in 1886 reforms had been made and some work had been done to build new houses, but the area was still a distinctly Irish part of the city. The men had earlier found work as navvies, labourers or coal heavers. But when Jimmy grew up there were other opportunities. The Waverly railway station had been built in 1844 and the nearby Waverly market was Edinburgh's equivalent to Covent Garden in London or Les Halles in Paris. This made it natural for Irish men in the Old Town to look for work in the transport trades.

And this is where Jimmy found a job as a vanman. This means he drove around with a horse-drawn covered wagon delivering goods, sometimes farm produce to or from the Waverly market or perhaps goods that had arrived by rail or were to be loaded on a train. He might also have driven his wagon out to Leith, which was Edinburgh's most important harbour. The Irish community was also strong in Leith and the Irish dominated the fish trade.

The history professor Robert Morris in Edinburgh explained to me what Jimmy's job as a vanman, as opposed to an ordinary driver, tells us about him. Firstly, that he was good with horses. Secondly, and more importantly, that he was trusted to take other people's goods out into the streets of Edinburgh. He must also have been able to handle records, lists and documents like receipts and paperwork for railway transport. Possibly he was also trusted to handle money on behalf of the owners of the goods. Jimmy, at eighteen, might not have been in charge of the wagon but

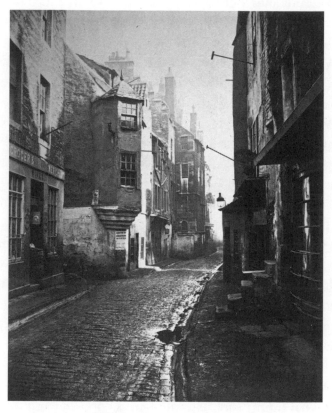

Cowgate in Edinburgh's Old Town was one of the areas where Irish immigrants settled.

would have been the driver's helper. But all this still points to him being a bright young lad, looking beyond the traditional jobs taken by men in Edinburgh's Little Ireland. It also fits in well with the duties he later had in the army during the war in 1914, when he was in charge of the officers' mess wagon and its supplies of food and drink.

Beside work there was football. Boys played (and still play) football in the park called The Meadows, just south of the narrow streets of the Old Town. This is where Edinburgh's top football clubs, The Hearts of Midlothian and The Hibernian, started playing. Their first derby match took place in The Meadows in 1875. In the early years of the 20th century, when Jimmy was a teenager, football was the dominating sport in working-class Scotland. Tens of thousands of spectators came to watch important matches, travelling to away games on special trains.

I do not know to which club Jimmy was drawn, but my first guess must be The Hibernians, or The Hibs, because the club has its roots in the Irish community. It is easy to think of Jimmy as a devoted Hibs fan, one of 30,000 spectators in the Ibrox Stadium in Glasgow in 1902, when his team beat Rangers 2–0 in the semi-final of the Scottish cup. With this win The Hibs qualified for the final against Celtic, the Glaswegian team that was supported by the city's big Irish community.

The papers wrote it up as an "all Irish" final. The great match was to have been played at Ibrox on 12 April, but it was postponed after a stand at Ibrox collapsed the week before, during the match between Scotland and England. Twenty-five spectators died and over 500 were injured. The cup final was moved to Celtic Park, giving Celtic the advantage of playing on its home ground.

On top of that several Hibs players were injured. But manager Paddy Cannon prepared his team well, keeping the players away from the pubs, and giving them milky cocoa to drink instead of alcohol.

Celtic were the favourites but Hibs won the final 1–0. The players and the supporters returned home by train, got off at Haymarket station and paraded the trophy along Princes street. Fifteen-year-old Jimmy Coyle must have been happy.

Forwards into the war

⊜ ALBERT ⊜

The players who earned a medal

Players in F.C. 02 Schedewitz were called into several different regiments and army units when Germany mobilized. More players probably joined the IR133 than any other unit because this regiment had its barracks in Zwickau, next to Schedewitz. Many of these players must have done their two years of national service there, or they were still in the regiment when war broke out. There is a group photograph of 30 members of the club, taken in 1911. Two of the players in the picture wear uniform. It must have been impossible, or at least very difficult, for a soldier to be a member of one of the club's teams or to come to a meeting because the soldiers seem to have had so little time off. They were even ordered to march to church on Sundays. Therefore it is not likely that the players in uniform in the picture came from a regiment far away. They probably were in IR133.

It is possible to estimate how many of the players were in IR133 when they went into the war. Another sports club in the town, the track and field club Turnverein Schedewitz, erected a memorial giving the names of the members who were killed in the war. There are 21 names carved into the stone and there are also the names of the regiments where they served. Five of the track and field athletes belonged to IR133, more than any other regiment. If this proportion was typical for young men in Schedewitz, then four of the 18 football players that the club lost would have been in IR133.

And four of the 18 names are in surviving lists of names of soldiers in the regiment. These lists are in the Sächsisches Staatsarchiv in Dresden. They list the names of non-commissioned officers and soldiers who have been decorated or have been recommended for decoration. There are several hundred names in these lists, but this is still just a small portion of all the names of the soldiers in the regiment. For most of them no information has survived.

I found information for two of the four players in F.C. 02 Schedewitz which persuaded me they were in IR133.

The first player was Alfred Lippold. He played at outside right in the club's second team during the 1912–1913 season, when the team scored 56 goals in nine games. On 28 November 1914 he was recommended for the Iron Cross, Second Class. The fights where he distinguished himself took place on 2 September at Somme-Py, some 120 miles east of Paris and around 8 September at Virty-le-François, which is about 40 miles to the south and a little closer to Paris.

Alfred Lippold was severely wounded during the fight at Vitry-le-François. A piece of shrapnel hit him in the thigh. It seems unlikely that he came back to the regiment. He died on 15 June 1915, according to the football club's Gedenktafel, which is a page in the 1927 Club history, giving the names of the 19 members who were killed in the war. Alfred Lippold has no registered war grave. He probably died in a hospital, possibly in Zwickau where many of the regiment's wounded soldiers were taken. He is not to be found in the lists of names on war memorials in Saxony, but he is mentioned in the list of soldiers who were decorated.

The other football player from Schedewitz who I found in IR133 was Albert Schmidt. He was a soldier in the first company, first battalion and he played inside right in the third team during the 1912–1913 season. No match results for the third team have survived. The club history just says all teams were very successful. Albert was a bugler and Gefreiter, the equivalent of Lance Corporal. He was an experienced soldier who had done well and had been promoted. He might even have decided to stay for a third year in the regiment. If so, he would have joined the army in 1911. I cannot resist looking at the two uniformed soldiers in the 1911 group photograph of players and think that one of them might be Albert.

Albert Schmidt is also mentioned in two lists. First he was recommended for the Iron Cross, Second Class, on 25 November 1914. The fight where he distinguished himself took place on 28 September near Moumelon-le-Grand, some 200 kilometres east of Paris. He is also on the list of soldiers who were decorated.

With this information I have chosen to follow Albert Schmidt through the war to Christmas, when his regiment took part in the Christmas Truce and he got the chance to kick a football together with the Scots.

 JIMMY

From Africa to Glasgow

I do not know why Jimmy Coyle decided to join the Argyll and Sutherland Highlanders. It might have been by chance or he might have chosen the regiment. The reason could have been that he happened to meet a persuasive recruitment agent. The regiment's recruiting area was away to the west of Edinburgh, but the agents are said to have felt free to work where they wanted. They were paid for each man they recruited and that would have been a good reason for an agent to try his luck in Edinburgh's Irish Old Town. Young Irish men who felt they were not accepted in Scotland were known to join the army to break out of their isolation.

The Argyll and Sutherland Highlanders, the regiment that Jimmy Coyle signed for in 1905, was then only 24 years old. It was a product of the reformation of the army in 1881, when several regiments that had only one battalion were amalgamated into new regiments. The battalions in these new regiments took turns to serve out in the vast British Empire. The new regiments also had units for reservists – soldiers who had served their time but were to be called up if need be – and Territorial units – soldiers who had joined for local duties only. Soldiers from both of these groups joined the active battalions after war broke out in 1914.

Thus two old regiments came together to form the Argyll and Sutherland Highlanders. They were the 91st Argyllshire Regiment, which became the first battalion of the new regiment, and the 93rd

Sutherland Highlanders, which became the second battalion. But the soldiers kept the old names and preferred to call their units simply the 91st and the 93rd. When they mentioned their battalions they usually said "the Regiment". This explains why Jimmy Coyle was captain of "the regimental football team", the battalion's team that played in the army cup. The old regiments kept their identities but soldiers often moved between the battalions.

So did Jimmy Coyle. I have not seen his service record, but other sources lead me to think that he was first sent to the 91st when he joined in 1905. This battalion at that time served in Scotland. Then I think he was sent out to the 93rd, which served in India up to 1907 and then went to South Africa. He possibly joined the 93rd during 1907–1909, when around 400 soldiers came to the battalion from Scotland.

This was after the Boer war in South Africa, but the soldiers' service was still demanding. There were marches and exercises, but there was also time for sport. The 93rd won the South African Army Football Championship both in 1908 and 1909.

Football was a major sport in the battalion and in the army. The 93rd won the first Army Cup in 1889, and reached the final again in 1891, but lost. During its service in India the 93rd won several football tournaments. Jimmy Coyle must have felt at home and possibly his strength as a footballer helped him advance through the ranks.

The 93rd left South Africa after 18 years service abroad and arrived in Glasgow on 28 January 1910. They marched in deep snow to Maryhill Barracks in the northern part of the city. The regimental history says that the battalion "now settled down to train itself for that European struggle, which all thinking soldiers and sailors, and most politicians, knew to be inevitable in the not far distant future."

The soldiers were given new equipment and they were sent on marches, exercises and manoeuvres together with other battalions. They also took part in parades, such as at the coronation of King George V in London in June 1911. When the king visited Edinburgh later in the summer, the 93rd lined Princes street and was guard of honour at St Giles' Cathedral, at Edinburgh Castle and at Holyrood Palace; all situated in the Old Town where Jimmy Coyle had grown up.

Jimmy's attention seems to have been divided between his soldier duties and football. During the years before the war he was captain of the regimental (i.e. the battalion's) football team.

In the autumn of 1911 the newspaper *Airdrie and Coatbridge Advertiser* wrote that the 93rd was among the favourites to win the Army Cup. The towns Airdrie and Coatbridge are situated east of Glasgow, some 15 miles from Maryhill Barracks. The reason this local newspaper mentioned the 93rd's football team was that the amateur football team of the Airdrie IOGT Lodge had been to the barracks to play the 93rd. This match took place on Saturday 11 November and the Lodge team lost 2–1 after the soldiers had scored in the last minutes of the game. The paper wrote:

"Although defeated by such a narrow margin, they [the Lodge team] are in no way discouraged, as the team of the Argyll and Sutherland Highlanders are now fancied strongly for the Army Cup."

The report went on to say that the game "was voted one of the stiffest encounters that has been seen on the Garrison pitch at Maryhill for years."

So the 93rd, one of the strongest teams in the army, chose to play the team of a rural IOGT lodge as they prepared themselves to win the cup. They won the match, but not really convincingly. Does that indicate that the standard of army football was rather low, on the level with a bunch of enthusiastic lodge members? Possibly, but it could just as well indicate that the lodge team played good football. The newspaper report says that their next match was at Hampden Park, the home of Queens Park, the amateur club that started football in Scotland. At this time Queens Park was no longer one of Scotland's strongest sides, but it still played in the first division of the Scottish League.

I have been told that the records of the 1911-1912 Army Cup have not survived. What is known is that the 93rd did not reach the final. The regimental history does not mention the Army Cup, so I conclude that the team was not successful.

The Airdrie players seem to have been impressed by Jimmy Coyle's play in the match at Maryhill and they seem to have told their friends at home about him. Or it could have been Jimmy who asked the Aridrie players for an opportunity to join a team. Whatever happened, contacts must have been taken, because in December Jimmy signed for the club Albion Rovers in Coatbridge. This was a professional club near the bottom of the second division of the Scottish League. There was no third division, so the Rovers were at the bottom of the bottom. The football reporter of the *Coatbridge Express* wrote on 15 November: "Things are desperate for the Rovers." A few weeks earlier he had written: "The Rovers have seldom given such a miserable display. The forwards were palpably weak, their efforts at goal being extremely feeble."

The football team of the 93rd played both in the Army
Cup and in civilian competitions and leagues. This
picture shows the team for the 1911–1912 season.

The team captain Jimmy Coyle is to the right of the
goalkeeper in the back row.
(Argyll and Sutherland Highlanders)

Jimmy Coyle got his first chance on the Rovers team in a league game against Dumbarton on 30 December 1911. Dumbarton won 2–0. Jimmy was mentioned by *Coatbridge Express* only in the line-up, as inside left. Next he played in the same position in an exhibition match on 2 January against Motherwell from the first division. The Rovers lost 7–1. Jimmy's third match for the Rovers, again as inside left, was a league game against Leith on 6 January. This time the *Coatbridge Express* reporter was pleased. "The activity of the Rovers forwards was most refreshing," he wrote. And the Rovers won, 1–0. So it seems Jimmy Coyle had been able to add some strength to the Rovers' attack.

After that Jimmy Coyle was not reported to have played any more games for the Rovers. The reason could of course be that the club did not think he was good enough. It could also be that he could not get away from his duties in the regiment. He might have been in a group of soldiers from the 93rd who were sent away for training in the south of England at the end of January. Then in April the battalion moved from Maryhill Barracks to Fort George, near Inverness on the east coast of Scotland.

While they were there the battalion team took part in civilian competitions under the name 93rd Highlanders. A writer in the regimental magazine summed up the 1912–1913 season as "hardly ...satisfactory". He wrote that forwards needed to be sharper and that "too many opportunities of scoring were missed." In the Highland League the soldiers were seventh out of nine teams with four wins and seven defeats. They reached the finals of two cup tournaments, but lost both. The most painful defeat came in the Elginshire cup against Buckie Thistle from the costal town of Buckie, east of Inverness. 93rd Highlanders "had

The soldiers' legs and feet were the Army's most important means of transportation. That is why the soldiers were constantly out on marching exercises. The picture shows the 93rd marching in Scotland before the war. (Argyll and Sutherland Highlanders)

all the best of the game," the regimental magazine reported, but still lost 3–1. The local newspaper *Banffshire Advertiser* reported that the soldiers were powerful but that the Thistle players were smart. It was "a victory for brains before beef."

So Jimmy Coyle's professional football career was cut short. He went on soldiering. The 93rd had a new organization with four companies instead of eight and the battalion was given new rifles. British soldiers were famous for shooting quickly and accurately. The musketry training required soldiers to hit a 12 inch target at 300 yards with at least 15 bullets in one minute. Some soldiers were said to score nearly twice as many hits. During the war British soldiers fought with many such powerful volleys, called mad minutes.

But Jimmy had also other things on his mind. On 24 December 1912 he married Nellie Johnson in Stirling. Their first child, Doreen Agnes Norrie, was born in Fort George on 5 October the following year.

⊜ ALBERT ⊜

A short march to the train

Albert Schmidt's first march in the war was one of the shortest. On 9 August 1914 the IR133 had a solemn service in the barrack yard. After that the soldiers in Albert's battalion marched out. They walked a mile or so to the railway. Albert was a bugler, so he might have been with the regimental musicians in the front.

A photographer took a picture of the band from a window overlooking Werdauer Street, at the bottom of the hill where the barracks are situated. The picture shows a fine summer's day. Most gentlemen wore straw hats. People lined the street. In some places spectators at the back had to look over or between four other people. Two women sat in an open window across the street. The slope by the street leading down from the barracks formed a natural grandstand, with a hundred spectators. At the back, by the stone wall, a man waved his hat. On the near side of the street, with his back to the camera, a man stretched to see over the heads of those in front. In a picture that must have been taken a few minutes later (see pages 36-37), when the fourth company marched by, he is seen eagerly waving his hat. Did he see a friend among the soldiers? Did he see his son?

The marching does not look like a festival. There is no sign of cheering. People in the pictures seem to watch the soldiers in silence.

Most soldiers in the German army were conscripts. Men in Germany were on national service from the year they were 17 years old until they were 45. Between the age of 20 and 28 most of them were in the army, first for two years active service, then in the reserve. But only about one half of German men did active service when their turn came.

War article 8, one of 28 ground rules of the armed forces, dealt with those who tried to avoid being called for active service. Men who cut off a hand or injured themselves in other ways were sent to prison together with anyone who helped. A man was not allowed to pay someone else to take his place in the forces. These rules were doubtless there because they were needed.

Also older men, who belonged to units set up for home defence could be called in and sent to the fronts, which was what happened during the war.

Soldiers in the reserve were called to exercises and also to one-day controls twice a year, when soldiers must come to their regiments. Military discipline was maintained, even at a distance. The soldier's most important duty was to report his address so that the army could reach him to call him in. A soldier who moved must report his new address within 14 days and a soldier who moved between military districts must report both to the old and the new district.

Also men living abroad must report their addresses so that

On 9 August 1914 the IR133 marched from their barrack square
to the train in Zwickau. A man (with his back to the camera)

waved his hat when the fourth company passed. Did he see a friend? Or did he see his son? (Norbert Peschke)

their military authorities back home in Germany could reach them in case of mobilization. The system proved efficient. Around 1 August trains and ships in Britain and across the Channel were crowded with German men who hurried home to their military units. During the Christmas Truce, the British soldiers met several Germans who had worked in England or Scotland before the war and even men who had grown up there, but who had done national service in Germany.

During one week from the first day of mobilization on 2 August, Germany's standing army grew from 700,000 soldiers, men who were doing their active national service, to 3.8 million. Of those, 2 million were sent to the fronts in the East and in the West.

Orders were issued to the reservists to carry food for one day when they joined their regiments and also to bring suitable packing for their civilian clothes, which were to be sent back home. The rules added: "If possible, [bring] no bowler hats."

Soldiers who left their regiments after their two years of active national service were replaced successively in the spring and the autumn. The majority of soldiers in a unit had always had some training. Because Albert Schmidt was a Gefreiter (Lance Corporal) he must have been one of the most experienced soldiers and he had probably done most of his active national service when war broke out. He could have been a reservist, but he was probably not because most of the soldiers in the regiment who went into the war in August were on active service.

The IR133 received the order to mobilize late in the evening on 1 August. That meant reservists were called in. They came, happy and singing, according to the officer Johannes Niemann, who wrote the regiment's war history, *Das 9. Königlich Sächsische Infanterie-Regiment Nr. 133 – im Weltkrieg 1914–18*, published in 1969. At the outbreak of war he was a young officer in the 9th Company. This company belonged to the Third Battalion, where Johannes Niemann also served as communications officer.

Johannes Niemann as a young officer. (From the 1968 BBC documentary "Christmas Day Passed Quietly")

The order to mobilize reached him when he was attending a war college in Danzig. He hurried back to his regiment in Zwickau and was immediately sent out into the country to collect a string of horses. He was given a detachment of reservists, who had never held a horse before. They could not calm the unruly horses, but with the assistance of a farmer Johannes Niemann managed to bring his herd into the barrack yard. This was the only small mishap during mobilization that Johannes Niemann mentioned in his book.

He wrote nothing about the regiment's departure from Zwickau, but another Saxon officer has told this story with many details. This officer published a book in 1915 about the first months of the war, but he did not give his name or the name of his regiment.

They left in the evening. He saw silent and painful farewells in dark corners at the station, a last embrace, a last pressure of the hand, but "those who were going away glowed from a pure

Dinner or lunch was ready at the stations when the troop trains stopped on their way to Germany's borders in the east and in the west. This picture shows Saxon soldiers washing before they went to eat. There were also barbers on hand. (From the book *Sachsen in grösser Zeit*)

eagerness, like a fire, to go against the enemy, towards victory."

A trumpet signal sounded, the signal to board, and the train started to move, slowly. "The great tension of nerves gave vent in a thundering 'Hurrah!' that came from a thousand throats, refusing to end."

The soldiers saw the lights of the station disappear in the August night. The worst was over, the farewells to the family, to home. The soldiers on the train fell silent and they realized that they were tired. The last couple of days had been hectic to get everything ready: men, horses, weapons, equipment, training of reservists. Now, their bodies took back what had been taken from them and the soldiers fell asleep.

When IR133 left Zwickau the soldiers did not know where their train was heading whether to the east to fight against Russians or to the west to fight against Frenchmen. Soon they saw that they were heading westwards. The journey went "past waving people and in beautiful sunshine," Johannes Niemann wrote.

The anonymous Saxon officer, who was also heading west, had more to tell. He described how well the men were taken care of on their way to the war. When they stopped at a station to eat, food halls were ready for them. There were hand basins with soap and towels and there were also barbers ready for a haircut or a shave at low prices. The men's food was excellent, like the officers', who were served in a special pavilion. As gifts the officers received imported cigars "of frightful blackness and size". After the meal there was time to write a short greeting to the people at home. Then sounded the signal to board.

They kept going westwards. When they passed Wartburg, known as the place where Martin Luther threw his inkpot at the Devil, "from the throats of several hundred enthusiastic German warriors flowed his old and always new song of protest, 'A Mighty Fortress is Our God' out into the flowering land."

When they stopped at stations the soldiers exchanged cheers and "Auf Wiedersehen!" with people who stood waving. Young girls in traditional dress and boy scouts offered lemonade in bowls and buckets. They were quickly emptied; the heat was sultry. The soldiers sang to thank them.

Next day started with a call: "The Rhine!" This river had a special, almost mythological, meaning for the soldiers, "the most German of all rivers, which we will protect together with all the other hundreds of thousands who march out."

The song 'Die Wacht am Rhein' was a second national anthem. It was one of the songs that sounded from the German trenches at Christmas.

But at that time the river Rhine did not mark the border between France and Germany. After the war between Prussia and France in 1870–1871, Alsace and Lorraine belonged to Germany and young men from these provinces were called into the German army.

The train ran over the bridge and the soldiers saw that it was guarded with machine-guns. IR133 travelled the same way, first down along the Rhine, then up along the river Moselle. Both regiments were bound for Speicher in der Eifel, not more than a village, which is situated just over ten miles from the border with Luxemburg.

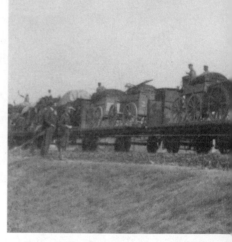

Speicher was one of many stations in western Germany which had been prepared to receive

Thousands of troop trains took Germany's soldiers to the frontiers after mobilization. This picture

regiments and their transport for a few days or weeks. It was the military authorities that decided where German railways were built. There were lines that were not needed for ordinary passenger traffic or by industry for freight. At the station in Speicher the military had extra long platforms built. They were there to make it possible to unload quickly the material brought by the troop trains.

When Germany mobilized, the army followed a logistics plan that had been prepared long before and was constantly reviewed and changed, to get the soldiers to their starting points in the east and in the west. Most transports went to the west. During 6–12 August 550 trains passed over the Rhine bridges every day. It took 6,010 railway carriages in 140 trains to carry one army corps and there were three corps in the German Third Army, to which IR133 belonged. All in all one and half million soldiers were brought to the borders of France, Luxembourg and Belgium where they readied themselves to attack.

Albert Schmidt's Regiment IR133 seems to have reached Speicher on 11 August. They were in the Eifel Mountains and the road from the railway

shows IR133 on their way west to the border with Luxembourg.
(Lorentz Zentgraf)

to their first billets in a village was uphill. This march in the hot weather was the soldiers' first test. They carried their ammunition pouches and their backpacks in a harness made of leather. During demanding trial marches before the war lots of soldiers could not keep up with their units and they fell behind. Therefore the army slimmed the pack. For example the lining was taken out of the overcoat, but the whole equipment still weighed almost 30 kilos with rifle, entrenching tool and bayonet, and their uniforms were made of wool. This proved too much for many of the regiment's reservists. Perhaps they had not done much marching in recent years. They fell at the roadside.

The regiment started to move slowly to the west and a few days later, on 18 August, they crossed the border into Luxembourg.

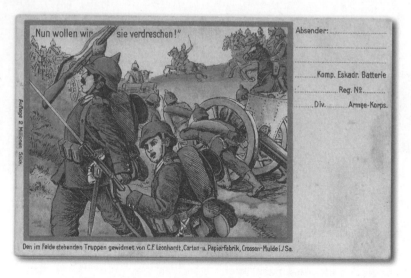

"Now we will give them a good thrashing!" is the text of this soldier's card, printed in millions. (Norbert Peschke)

⊜ JIMMY ⊜

First over the Channel

Jimmy Coyle's battalion, the second battalion in the Argyll and Sutherland Highlanders, or the 93rd as the soldiers preferred to call it, was in the first group of fighting units that came to France after mobilization.

They went ashore in Boulogne on Tuesday 11 August. A guard of honour consisting of a detachment of older French soldiers from the home defence greeted them. Cheering spectators pressed the soldiers and were in their way when they formed up on the quay. It was mostly women, children and older men. The younger men had already left to join their military units.

The battalion had received the order "Mobilize" on Wednesday afternoon 5 August, the day after the British declaration of war against Germany. The 93rd were stationed at Fort George on the eastern coast of Scotland.

Although the battalion was a part of Britain's standing professional Army it was not ready to enter the war. It needed more horses, more materiel and more men. Seven-hundred reservists were needed to bring the battalion up to regulation strength, just over 1,000 men. The reservists were either professional soldiers who had served out their contracts, or they were soldiers who joined the professionals for six months training and then signed for seven years in the reserve.

Britain's mobilization, like Germany's, was regulated and planned. The name of the planning manual was the *War Book*, a dictionary with thousands of pages with plans for several possible conflicts analysed by experts. There was among other things a list of all horses and transport lorries in the country and a plan for railway traffic. It is wrong to think that the British improvised while the methodical Germans followed their mobilization plan. But at least some important points in the British plan proved to be not as well thought out as the German plan, at least in Jimmy Coyle's battalion.

Officials in British civil and military authorities now took out their relevant pages in the *War Book*. They entered "Germany" in the designated space in telegrams concerning the declaration of war, which lay ready to be sent out. But for the staff in Fort George one word in the telegrams was enough: "Mobilize".

When the reservists started coming to the 93rd it immediately became evident that the *War Book*'s plans had proved inadequate in some important aspects. Several new soldiers walked barefoot. The boots that they had been given were too small. When they left active service a few years earlier their sizes of boots had been noted. Then, when they came back, they were given a pair of boots of the size given in the list. But something had happened to their feet during the years when they had been civilians. The boots did not fit and there were evidently not enough boots of the right size.

This was a serious problem. The soldiers had not many means of transport other than their feet. They were meant to march through the coming war. Boots that did not fit were just as serious as a modern army being given tyres that did not fit the wheels of its road vehicles.

Henry Hyslop was one of the company commanders in the 93rd. He kept a diary during the war. He solved the boot problem by ordering soldiers with boots that did not fit to sit down in a ring. They sent their boots along the ring until most of them had found boots that they could march in.

At the same time as the reservists came the horses, picked up out in the country. The 93rd had 63 horses when the battalion went off to the front in France. During mobilization they were picketed on the cricket ground in Fort George and "look[ed] a very likely lot," Henry Hyslop wrote. But the horses could not pull. The reason was that their harnesses did not fit. A comparison, again, with an army today would be that the available engines did not fit the transport lorries.

This was the reason why the battalion's trains were late when they started from Fort George for Southampton in southern England on Sunday night 9 August. It took them one night and one day to reach the harbour and it was a horrid journey. There were many people waiting at stations to wish the soldiers good luck and give them presents, but the soldiers were not properly fed. Not even at home in Scotland and England could the Army provide sufficient food for its soldiers.

The drummer Charles Ditcham was 18 years old just before war broke out. He described what food was given to the soldiers for the journey. It was one tin of bully beef, like corned beef, and four biscuits, army biscuits that resemble dog biscuits. Ten men and their equipment were crammed into each compartment. There was no toilet on the train, nor were there enough toilets for two companies at stations where they stopped.

When the train stopped at stations the battalion sent telegrams ahead, asking for boiling water for tea to be ready when they were passing. But not even the officers knew what route the train was to take, so the battalion could only send a telegram at the last minute, and when the train came, nothing was ready. Not until they got to Rugby, two thirds of the way, was there tea for the soldiers.

The officers in Henry Hyslop's train were better off because the mess sergeant was on that train. He had brought a good store of food and drink. The mess sergeant was 28-year-old Jimmy Coyle. He started serving as soon as the train passed Inverness, some ten miles from Fort George. For this Henry Hyslop gave him a favourable mention in his diary.

When they came to Southampton the 450 soldiers on Jimmy Coyle's train were ordered at once to board a cattle ship. This became another trying journey. Half of the men were below deck, where there was not even room to lie down. The other half were left on deck, so they could lie down and get some sleep. It was a fine night, but chilly.

Some of the officers found a small cabin, which they shared, others lay down on the bridge. Jimmy Coyle got another favourable mention in Henry Hyslop's diary for serving a meal for the officers, who took turns to eat in the small cabin.

The cattle ship was put to sea on Monday night 10 August, just two hours after the train had come to Southampton. Crews on other ships cheered the soldiers. When the ship had left the harbour the captain opened his sealed orders and found that they were bound for Boulogne.

They sighted the French coast the next morning at seven o'clock. "The ubiquitous Sergt. Coyle produced breakfast" for the officers. An hour or so later a pilot came aboard to steer the ship through the newly laid minefield outside the harbour. The first fighting soldiers of the British Expeditionary Force (BEF) went ashore in Boulogne around nine o'clock that morning.

Led by their pipers the Scots marched to their billets in barracks in the city. The officers had taught the men to answer the crowd's "Vive l'Angleterre!" with a just as cheerful "Vive la France!" The soldiers' kilts were the talk of the town.

The rest of the battalion arrived during the following days and the soldiers were put to work pitching tents and setting up camp for units that kept coming to Boulogne. The Scots were also sent to the harbour to help unload equipment and stores. There was also time for exercises for the reservists. On many mornings officers led their soldiers to the beach for a swim. The mayor supplied bathing costumes.

Not until more than a week later did the 93rd receive orders to march to the station to be taken by rail to the front. The crowds along the way gave presents to the soldiers. There were rosaries, crosses and rosettes in the French colours. In return the soldiers gave away their shoulder badges. The women wore them as brooches and the men wore them in their caps.

Before the battalion left Boulogne the officers had bought a horse and cart, which they loaded with a good supply of tinned food and many cases of whisky. It was to be driven by Jimmy Coyle, who had experience handling perishable goods from his days as a vanman in Edinburgh.

The 93rd was sent to Valenciennes, some 100 miles upcountry, near the border with Belgium. They got there after a "horrid" journey, according to Lance Corporal Adam McLachlan in A

The Scots of the Argyll and Sutherland Highlanaders were the first fighting soldiers who came ashore in the harbour in Boulogne. Their kilts were the talk of the town. Soldiers gave away their regimental badges to ladies who wore them as brooches. (Taylor Library)

Company, who later wrote about his time in the war.

The battalion became a part of the 19th brigade. The other battalions in this brigade were the first battalion Scottish Rifles (also called The Cameronians), the first battalion Middlesex Regiment and the second battalion, Royal Welch Fusiliers. The 19th Brigade was not attached to any larger unit, but was moved around as required.

At 11 o'clock in the morning on Sunday 23 August the 93rd marched out of Valenciennes; out into the war.

The soldiers wore tartan kilts, but over the kilts they wore khaki coloured protective aprons. An officer wrote that he thought the aprons were stupid, "stiff, cumbersome and ugly". The kilts were made of wool and were also lined with wool or linen. The soldiers wore boots and knee-high socks. They wore their kilts all the year round and in the winter walked with bare knees in muddy trenches.

Their coats were of khaki coloured wool and looked more like jackets, that were cut short at the front to make room for sporrans, the traditional small bags that were part of the uniforms, but not worn in the war. Instead there was a pocket at the front of the apron. On their heads the soldiers wore glengarry caps with two ribbons at the back and a red and white chequered band all around. This was worn only by the Argyll and Sutherland Highlanders in recognition of their conduct during the battle of Balaclava during the Crimean war, when the Scots formed "a thin red line" to hold off a Russian attack. In their caps they wore their regimental metal badge, which was the biggest in the Army. They had no helmets. These did not arrive until 1916.

The soldiers carried their equipment in harnesses made of

tightly woven cotton. At the front they wore two ammunition pouches. Their bayonet, water flask and entrenching tool were attached to their belts. On their backs they carried packs with things like overcoat, food, plate, and knife, fork and spoon. All in all they carried sometimes over 30 kilos of gear. The rifle weighed four or five kilos.

I have not found Jimmy Coyle's exact place in the battalion. Henry Hyslop wrote that he was mess sergeant, but there was no such position in the organizational table. It is clear he was with the transport. That meant he was often not in the trenches and his job was not to take part in attacks. The transport was often, if possible, sent away to safety when the battalion got ready to fight or risked being in a dangerous situation. This is probably one reason why he survived the war.

There is no information about how many of the soldiers, who came with the battalion to Boulogne in August 1914, were still there when the battalion returned to Scotland in May 1919. But there is a picture of soldiers in the Second Battalion, Royal Welch Fusiliers, who served through the war. This battalion was in the 19th brigade together with the 93rd in the beginning of the war. There are ten men in the picture, five of whom had positions behind the front. (The picture was taken after many soldiers had been demobbed and sent home. Also, a number of soldiers had surely been transferred to other units during the war, where they might have survived. But if the real number of men who served all through the war was 20 instead of 10, it is still only a few.) There is no reason to believe that more soldiers survived the war in the 93rd than in the Royal Welch Fusiliers.

And there is no doubt that Jimmy Coyle took part in the

fighting when he was needed. When the battalion was in a dangerous situation nobody could stay behind the front if they did not have jobs that needed to be done. Looking after the stores of the officers' mess was not such an important job. Jimmy Coyle's Military Medal shows that he took part in dangerous tasks, but some tasks were even more dangerous.

@ ALBERT @

Marching on

The American journalist E. Alexander Powell worked in Belgium in the autumn of 1914. He was correspondent for the *New York World*, one of the great newspapers of that time. He was invited to visit the German First Army that marched through Belgium towards France and he was impressed: "Far as the eye could see stretched solid columns of marching men, pressing westward, ever westward," he wrote. One of his hosts wanted to demonstrate the German artillery. Soldiers brought a gun into a field, aimed it at a windmill three miles away and hit it with the first shell.

These soldiers belonged to the German First Army, so Albert Schmidt was not there. But Alexander Powell would have witnessed the same striking power if he had been invited to the Third Army, where IR133 was one of the regiments, or to any of the other armies that attacked from the border with the Netherlands in the north to the Swiss border in the south.

The tramp of good German boots was heard on hundreds of roads. These boots were much sought after. Alexander Powell wrote that he had seen Belgian farmers risk their lives on a battlefield to take boots off dead German soldiers. And the soldiers seem to have had a doubly intimate relation with their boots. They gave them a pet name, "Knobelbecher". This is the word for a leather mug, used for throwing dice. But Knobel is also an old word for ankle.

The German army had detailed rules for marching and for soldiers' care of their feet. These regulations were important; elaborately developed and tested, like service manuals for troop transport vehicles in a modern army. Albert Schmidt's soldiers' book of rules, *Dienstunterricht des Königlich Sächsischen Infanteristen* and the supplementary reader *Der gute Kamerad* said that his feet were almost more important than his rifle. Success depends on the ability to march and "like everything else in the world this has to be learnt."

The first thing that the soldier had to learn was to look after his feet. Alexander Powell wrote that the soldier's feet did not belong to himself but belonged to the Emperor of Germany and that the Emperor expected these feet to be kept in perfect condition so that they could carry the soldier successfully through the fighting. The soldiers' books confirmed Powell's observation: "a soldier with bad feet is useless", and regulated the care of feet in detail.

The feet must be kept clean, washed if possible each day, especially in the summer and especially during hot days like there were in August 1914. The soldier must cut his toenails with scissors and scrape away corns with a knife, extremely

The American journalist Alexander Powell visited the German First
Army as it advanced through Belgium towards France. He wrote about
marching men "far as the eye could see..."
(Donald Thompson, from E. Alexander Powell's
book *Fighting in Flanders*)

carefully. If the feet become hard the soldier should soak them in
lukewarm soapy water. To make his feet strong the soldier shall
wash them with cold water or with "Branntwein" (schnapps).
Soldiers who have sweaty feet should bathe their feet often in
cold water, apply tallow and change socks or footcloths. *Der
gute Kamerad* sets down what responsibility a soldier has for his
sweaty feet. He shall care for them "like a mother cares for her
sick child".

Finally the soldiers' book gives the reader a piece of insider
advice, "even if it is difficult to believe": experienced soldiers

claim that they never get sore feet during a long march if they have fresh green leaves from a tree in their helmet or in their trouser pockets.

But there were also other instructions for care of the feet, which are easier to understand. These were about boots. *Der gute Kamerad* reminds the soldier that boots must fit and be comfortable. But this is not so much about the soldier's comfort but because "it is of vital importance for the ability to march."

For boots there were rules for the length (one breadth of thumb longer than the foot), the width (toes must not rub against each other) and the height of the leather upper (there must be room enough for the soldier to curl his toes). Soldiers were also told how to test boots: "Step up on a stool and jump off. If the boots do not press your feet they fit well."

Bootlegs must be wide enough for trouser legs to be tucked inside without pressing on the calves. "It is sign of serious disorder to use the bayonet to push trouser legs into tall boots." Then come rules for the heel (must not be unevenly worn) and the inner sole (nails from the outer sole must not penetrate). And lastly the book stresses that all this is not just good advice but orders. "Soldiers who do not immediately report such defects to their nearest commander are liable to be punished."

The army showed that it took regulations for shoes and feet seriously, that they were important, and that they were actually vital for success in the war. Alexander Powell saw shoemakers working in wagons during the march. He also reported that specialist pedicurists were on the staff of ambulances.

The British Army also had shoemakers and there were rules for the care of feet, but judging from the instruction books the German Army seems to have attached more importance to feet. The official British history of the war notes that under the severe conditions during the winter of 1914–1915 the soldiers were supposed to rub their feet with whale oil, but no whale oil reached the trenches for weeks "and worse than this there was a shortage of boots."

The German instruction books also had detailed rules for soldiers to keep healthy, which was also vital for their ability to march. The soldier must wash his hands and brush his teeth every day. He must often go for a swim, but not on a full stomach. He must keep his hair close-cropped. Alexander Powell saw an officer who stood by the marching columns together with a soldier carrying a tool that looked like horse-clipping machine. When the officer saw a soldier with too long hair he was pulled out of the column, the clipper was run over his head and he was sent running forward to re-join his company.

Alexander Powell also saw cooks in white aprons leaning out of their wagons, serving soup to the men, without them having to stop.

Marching was nothing like walking for pleasure, even if Johannes Niemann took time to admire the beautiful landscape when IR133 marched through Luxembourg. The soldiers' columns were regulated with 80 centimetres between the pack at the back of one soldier to the chest of the soldier that followed. They must keep pace and the correct length of step, but they had also some liberties during the march. They were allowed to carry their rifles on the shoulder or under the arm, they could talk and they could smoke. If they were given permission they could undo buttons in their coats and loosen their scarfs.

And they were allowed to sing. Or rather, they were ordered to sing. The lyrics of suitable songs were in their instruction books. Among the songs were 'Der gute Kamerad', 'Deutschland', 'Deutschland über Alles' and 'Die Wacht am Rhein'. Specially for the Saxons there was also 'Gott sei mit dir mein Sachsenland'. The soldiers' book *Der gute Kamerad* warned soldiers not to sing certain songs, most probably for obvious reasons. "The respectable soldier does not sing indecent or rude songs, they are strictly prohibited."

But good, patriotic songs give a good impression, the books stated. A column of singing straight-backed soldiers attracts attention from "old and young and from nice girls." I wonder if this was what the Saxons expected when they marched towards Belgium.

Real war

Graves at the roadside

Albert Schmidt's regiment entered the war without fighting. They made their first advance through Luxembourg on 18 August. They continued into Belgium the same day and walked westwards, towards the eastern shore of the river Meuse. The anonymous Saxon officer, who wrote more vividly in his book about the war than Johannes Niemann wrote in his book, tells how his regiment crossed the border to Belgium with a roaring "Hurrah!"

Both Johannes Niemann and the anonymous officer wrote that they saw traces of fighting when they marched into Belgium. The officer wrote that inhabitants had used trees and machinery from a factory to build barricades. Then German cavalrymen ordered Belgians, young and old, to clear away the obstacles to open the road.

The officer saw German graves, decorated with soldiers' helmets, swords or bayonets and with flowers. Johannes Niemann also wrote that the soldiers saw the graves. "They made many of us thoughtful."

This was not an exercise and it was not one of the many study tours that Germany's supreme commander had conducted with his top officers during the years. This was real war.

The regiment IR133 entered foreign territory in Luxembourg on the 17th day of war, counting from 2 August, the first day of mobilization. That left the German forces just another 25 days to force France to capitulate, according to the plan for the war. The day of victory was thus fixed at 12 September.

Germany's plan was to send most of her soldiers against France when the war started. This force was to secure an early victory in the west and then many soldiers could be sent to the east, against the Russians. With this strategy Germany would avoid conducting war on two fronts at the same time. What they had to do was to defeat France before Russia had time to fully mobilize her army.

In order to defeat France in a short time Germany had developed a plan not to attack France straight on in a westerly direction across the border between the countries. Instead the strongest forces would be sent through Belgium in order to attack France from the north, on her left flank in military parlance, or even from behind. An attack through Belgium would also avoid the strong French fortifications, such as Verdun.

But this plan also had drawbacks. The soldiers who were to attack France from the north must march a long way and it was going to be difficult to bring food and other supplies to them. The German First Army, making the widest swing through Belgium, had to walk over 200 miles from the railway stations at the German border to Paris. This army had 84,000 horses that needed almost 1,000 tons of fodder each day. As the army marched further away from the nearest usable railheads more fodder was needed just to bring forage to the frontline units. Furthermore an invasion of Belgium would increase the risk of Britain joining the war. Belgium was a neutral country and Britain guaranteed Belgium's neutrality. Britain used this argument when she declared war on Germany even if other reasons surely were more important, such as preventing Germany from dominating the Continent and seizing the Channel ports.

The German force that attacked France consisted of seven armies. The First Army started furthest to the north and was on the rim of the wheeling action. Inside the First Army was the Second Army and inside the Second Army was the Third Army, where Albert Schmidt's regiment IR133 belonged.

The IR133 belonged to the 89th brigade, which belonged to the 40th division, which belonged to the 19th army corps, commonly written XIXth corps. This was one of three army corps in the Third Army, which was a Saxon army.

There were three battalions in the regiment with four companies in each battalion. Albert Schmidt was in the first company, which was in the first battalion.

The anonymous Saxon officer wrote with many details about the march into Belgium. When officers sought billets for the night they were never on their own and they had sentries posted. The men were not allowed to walk alone in a town when they stopped for a break. The officer wrote about a transport that had been ambushed in a seemingly peaceful town: "of course there was a punishment."

The regiment later came to a big farm with many barns and the Germans demanded to be given billets for the night.

Albert Schmidt's regiment IR133 walked to the south through
France and fought several times against French soldiers. After 24

days of war the regiment was east of Paris. During this time the soldiers had only one day of rest. (Lorenz Zentgraf)

The officer wrote that the brothers who owned the farm looked at him hatefully. At first the brothers denied that they had any firearms, but the officer threatened to shoot them if German solders still found any weapons. Then the brothers came out with firearms and ammunition. "In order to save our tired men guarding them, I had the rascals locked into an empty firewood cellar after we had given them straw, blankets, bread, water and smoked meat." After that the officers dined on beef and noodles and a "really good draught beer which we had found in great quantity in the cellar."

On 22 August, four days after their entry into Belgium, the IR133's division had assembled just east of the river Meuse, near the city of Dinant. But before they got there, Albert Schmidt's battalion had been ordered to join another regiment. Together they were to attack the town of Hastière-par-delà. It is situated on the eastern shore of the Meuse, a few miles north of the border with France and in the town there was a bridge over the river. Here the river runs between high cliffs and dense forests so that the soldiers could only pass on the roads. When they came to Hastière-par-delà the soldiers saw that the bridge had been blown up. French soldiers shot at them from the other side of the river but a few patrols still managed to cross. Johannes Niemann quotes another officer in his book: "The town burned. Three franc-tireurs were shot." (The French word "franc-tireur" stands for a person who fights in a war but is not a soldier in the regular army, rather like a guerilla fighter, but this word was not used in 1914.)

This was 23 August, the height of what on the German side was called the war on franc-tireurs or sometimes Belgian and French atrocities against German soldiers. But in the countries at the other side of the conflict these events became known as German atrocities against civilians in Belgium and France.

The term "franc-tireur" stems from the war between France and Prussia in 1870-1871, when French irregular fighters attacked Prussian soldiers. Memories of these attacks were still alive in the German armies in 1914. Many of the officers who had reached high positions in 1914 had taken part in the war in 1870-1871. Among them was Max von Hausen, commander of the German Third Army, where Albert Schmidt was in the IR133. Commanders in the Third Army warned their soldiers that they could expect to be attacked by civilians in Belgium and France. This stood out as one of the dangers awaiting them as they marched into war.

Units of the Third Army had orders to punish communities where German soldiers were attacked or were thought to have been attacked by franc-tireurs. Villages and towns were pillaged and burnt and their inhabitants were killed or deported. A 2001 study concluded that about 6,500 civilians were killed in Belgium and France from August to October. The study lists events when German soldiers intentionally killed ten or more civilians. On 23 August there were 15 such events when a total of 1,212 civilians were killed. Nineteen of these civilians were killed in Hastière-par-delà, where Albert Schmidt's battalion was one of the units that took part in the fighting.

The fight went on all day. The civilian population was caught between the French and the German soldiers. The Germans accused the inhabitants of helping the French and therefore the town was punished. Among those who were shot to death were two ten-year-old boys.

The next day the rest of IR133 took part in a fight at the town of Haybes, where 61 civilians were killed and where German soldiers also used civilians as human shields.

The 2001 study also concluded that in most of these events it was not franc-tireurs who shot at the German soldiers. The fire came from French soldiers or from German soldiers who shot at each other in the darkness and the confusion. But a German officer, who wrote about the war, said that they could tell if the fire came from soldiers or civilians. The gunpowder in the soldiers' ammunition left thin, grey smoke whereas the smoke from civilians' rifles was densely brown.

Jimmy Coyle's battalion, the 93rd, also killed civilians, according to Frank Collier, one of the soldiers. He wrote about an occasion east of Paris in the beginning of September: "Previous to our moving off we shot a farmer and his son who claimed they were Swiss but who were caught signalling with heliograph from one of their hay loft windows." Frank Collier also wrote about an event, probably on 17 September: "...owing to the work of some spies (men and women who were promptly shot) our Brigade narrowly escaped having very severe casualties by heavy howitzer shelling..." None of these events are mentioned in the battalion's war diary.

In the evening after the fight in Hastière-par-delà Albert Schmidt's battalion assembled at a manor outside the town. While they waited for the bridge to be repaired they enjoyed food that they had found and requistioned. There was jam, pineapple, sekt (dry white wine), red wine and other delicacies. They could also reflect on their first fight. Nine soldiers had been killed, 145 were injured and two were missing.

The next afternoon they crossed the bridge and marched to the south through dense woods on the western side of the river Meuse. For several days they passed through villages that were burning after they had been hit by German artillery grenades. In one village the inhabitants had hoisted a white flag on the church tower. They crossed the border into France but they did not meet much resistance from French units. French equipment was spread along the road. They met refugees. On 27 August they found a barn where they could sleep and the transport reached them, bringing mail, the first they had received since they marched out into the war. Their own army corps came marching and the battalion could re-join their regiment.

◉ JIMMY ◉

The first day of the war

On Sunday 23 August, at noon, the soldiers in the 93rd heard the thunder of guns for the first time in this war. They were marching to the east near Valenciennes in France towards Mons in Belgium. The sound of the guns came from straight ahead.

A few days earlier the British Expeditionary Force (BEF) had assembled around Mons. The BEF was a comparatively small force with just over 160,000 men on 15 September. Both the French Army and the German Army in the west were about ten times as big.

The British prepared to move north in order to attack the

German forces that marched through Belgium and had now turned south. The attack was to be made together with the French Fifth Army, which was east of the BEF. The British force was almost at the extreme western end of the Allied forces and the 93rd was, together with the other three battalions of the 19th brigade, at the western end of the BEF. The plan was for the British to attack the western part of the German force that came from the north and to hit the Germans in their flank in a classic manoeuvre.

The French were already engaged in combat. The British were told that the French Fifth Army could not cross the river Sambre. Neither the British nor the French knew which opponent they faced. The German First Army and Second Army came from the north and from the northeast came the Third Army, where Albert Schmidt was in the 133rd regiment. It was 750,000 Germans against 350,000 British and French soldiers.

The 93rd reached the Belgian border on Sunday night. One company was ordered to the north, to the frontline, and some platoons were sent on outpost duty and to protect the brigade's ammunition transport. The rest of the soldiers lay down to sleep in a factory and the officers managed to get into a house where they could wash. The march from Valenciennes had been hot and dusty. The adjutant gave out maps of Belgium. The guns roared over towards Mons. Henry Hyslop wrote that "...we fully expect to be in the thick of it to-morrow".

They were awakened at midnight and prepared to march on. While they were by the roadside, waiting for orders, they could hear the thunder of the guns "...and not long after very distinct rifle fire made us rather sit up," Henry Hyslop wrote. Civilian refugees came along the road. There were also wounded British soldiers, some from other battalions in the Brigade. The soldiers told about intense fighting around Mons.

Not until seven o'clock on Monday morning 24 August came the order for the 93rd to march on. They walked to the east. The battalion was at the end of the brigade with one company acting as rear guard. They crossed the border to Belgium and continued towards the fighting around Mons, some 12 miles away. After less than a mile the marching column stopped. Then the brigade turned to the right, to the south.

Henry Hyslop wrote: "...it dawned on us that we were retiring from the Germans. This came as a great shock..."

Retiring they were indeed. This was the beginning of what would be known as the retreat from Mons. During this retreat the battalion was split into several groups who in vain tried to find each other. Some soldiers found themselves on a train that took them a hundred miles or so to central France. Not until 5 September could all soldiers get together again, all soldiers, that is, who had not been killed or wounded, gone missing or had become German prisoners. At that time the battalion found itself less than 20 miles from Paris.

The British soldiers around Mons defended themselves and halted the German forces. Germany had not expected such resistance. One German company commander, who survived this day, found that all the other three company commanders in his battalion had been killed. He wrote: "No sooner had we left the edge of the wood than a volley of bullets whistled past our noses and cracked into the trees behind. Five or six cries near me, five or six of my grey lads collapsed into the grass... The

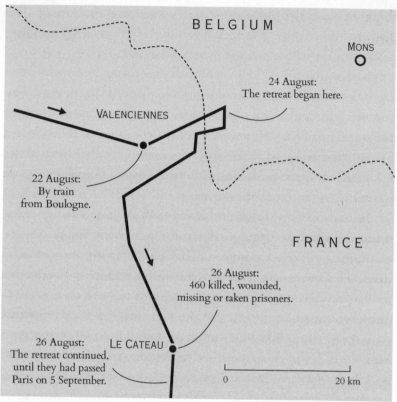

BELGIUM

MONS
O

24 August:
The retreat began here.

VALENCIENNES

22 August:
By train
from Boulogne.

FRANCE

26 August:
460 killed, wounded,
missing or taken prisoners.

26 August: LE CATEAU
The retreat continued,
until they had passed
Paris on 5 September.

0   20 km

"This came as a shock...", wrote the officer Henry Hyslop after the 93rd was ordered to turn to the south instead of marching towards the thunder of the guns around Mons. "...it dawned on us that we were retiring from the Germans."

firing seemed at long range. ...away in front a sharp, hammering sound, then a pause, then a more rapid hammering – machine-guns!" But this was not machine-guns, it was the rifle fire from the professional British soldiers.

This officer's regiment, with a regulation force of more than

3,000 soldiers, lost 500 men when they attacked the British. The British lost around 1,600, killed, wounded, missing or taken prisoner, and they managed to kill or wound an estimated 5,000 German soldiers.

All the time new German soldiers attacked the British until the British found themselves in a dangerous situation. This became even more dangerous when the French Fifth Army, to the east of the BEF, decided to retreat because they saw the German Third Army coming. The French force that was to the west of the 93rd also retreated. So the British had to join in the retreat. Historians who have written about the war also point out that the British supreme commander, John French, seems to have had a change of mind. Earlier his intention was to drive the German forces back to Germany. Now he seemed to be more concerned with protecting his expeditionary force. He did not trust the command of the French Fifth Army that had started retreating without consulting the command of the BEF. John French even contemplated withdrawing to the coast and building a defence there.

After the 93rd had broken off their march towards Mons and turned to the south, they crossed the border back into France at midday. Twice they were ordered to stop and dig defences against an attack from the north, but both times they were ordered to march on. Charles Ditcham has told how they marched "from here to there" and that he did not know why, "but all I do know I had sore feet."

The soldiers in the 93rd now saw German soldiers for the first time. The British artillery fired at the Germans and the Scots saw them flee. In the evening, the battalion came to the village of Eth on the French side of the border. They set up their defence in trenches that French soldiers had dug. The transport wagons came, pulled by worn out horses. The drivers, Jimmy Coyle might have been one of them, had been shown the wrong way and they had travelled between the German and the British lines. But they brought no food, just tea and biscuits.

One of the platoons, which had been on outpost duty returned late at night. In the morning this platoon had been given the task of protecting the brigade on the north side of the road towards Mons. The soldiers had come across a German infantry battalion, there had been a fight and there had been casualties. Private Thomas Rodger, 23 years old, and Private Cassidy were the first soldiers in the 93rd to be killed in the war. Another 13 soldiers had been wounded. Fortunately they were picked up by an ambulance from the cavalry.

So ended Monday 24 August, the battalion's first day at war. The day had started with what Henry Hyslop described as "...our one anxiety is to get forward..." It ended with "orders received that this position must be held at all costs," entered in the battalion war diary. The soldiers had been on their feet since soon after midnight, or they had lain, perhaps slept, at the side of a road. They had marched for 16 miles and dug trenches under a burning sun. In the evening they lay down in their trenches, or among sheaves of corn if they were lucky to be in the company in reserve. They were told to expect a German attack at any moment.

A half battalion

It was Tuesday 25 August. The 93rd found themselves in the village of Eth in France, just south of the Belgian border. The soldiers were allowed to rest until one o'clock at night. They had tea and biscuits. At three o'clock they stood in their trenches, ready to defend themselves against an attack, but a few hours later they were ordered to continue to the south. When they had left the village, the German artillery fired at their empty trenches and then the infantry attacked. All this took almost three hours, the British cavalry later reported to the Scots. It "...must have been of great value in our retirement," wrote Henry Hyslop.

The order was to get away from the Germans, to the south. Both men and horses were tired. The wagon that carried the officers' equipment got stuck where the road was waterlogged and the horses could not pull it out. The soldiers threw off valises to lighten the wagon, but the horses still could not pull it out. Then the soldiers cut the horses from the wagon and set fire to it. Among the luggage that was lost was the adjutant's chest, which was the battalion's office, where the war diary was kept. The diary that we can read today was reconstructed and written later and it was signed on 2 October.

Around midday the battalion had marched some 18 miles and had reached the village of Hussey. A German aeroplane followed them. The war diary tells that people in the village started cooking a meal for the soldiers. Adam McLachlan in A Company wrote that the soldiers tried to tend to their sore and swollen feet. But German artillery and German cavalry put a stop to all this. The battalion formed up for defence on a ridge and after a few hours they were on their way again.

They walked to the south. Some men walked barefoot because they could not get their feet into their boots. It started to rain. It was the first rain they had had since they came to France, wrote Frank Collier, also in A Company. They were wet through because many had thrown their coats away a few hours earlier. In the evening the battalion squeezed into a factory in the town of Le Cateau and they tried to get some sleep. They had marched 30 miles during the day.

The 19th Brigade, where the 93rd was one of the battalions, at this time belonged to the Second Army Corps in the BEF. The general in command was Horace Smith-Dorrien. He had orders to continue retiring to get as far away as possibly from the Germans. The plan was to reach a natural obstacle, like a river, where they could build a stable defence. But the general came to realize that the soldiers could not keep on marching after what they had been through on Tuesday. The war diary of the 93rd says the men had had a "very trying march in rain." They had walked with their heavy packs on cobblestoned roads, many had sore feet and they had not had enough to eat or drink. The reservists, who had joined the battalion a few weeks earlier, could not cope with long, demanding marches.

Horace Smith-Dorrien knew that the soldiers in the 93rd had had a difficult day. In the evening he received a message from First Corps, which were at the village of Landrecies, some 20 miles to the east. The First Corps asked for help to fight off a surprise attack. One possibility would have been to send the 19th

Brigade, but General Smith-Dorrien answered that the brigade would be "unable to reach Landrecies in a useful state." The soldiers were exhausted.

At the same time the staff of the Second Corps realized that the Germans had come further south than expected. In the small hours of Wednesday 26 August, Horace Smith-Dorrien came to the conclusion that it was too late to decamp and resume the retreat to the south. He decided that his force must stay and defend themselves. He reported this to a general in the British headquarters. He spoke from a railway station where they had found a telephone connection. The general in the headquarters answered that there would be no help for the Second Corps and that there would be a new Sedan. He referred to the battle of Sedan in 1870, when the Prussian army beat the French army and took 100,000 prisoners.

While the general in the headquarters said this, Horace Smith-Dorrien heard a thud and then another. "It's too late. It's started," he said.

The battle at the town of Le Cateau on 26 August was the BEF's second major fight during the first week of the war. What the Second Corps achieved that day was that it still existed when evening came. But by then 8,000 soldiers had been killed, wounded or were missing. For the soldiers in the 93rd the battle of Le Cateau was their first major fight in this war. Forty soldiers were killed, 114 were wounded and 311 were reported missing after the fight. Many of the missing had been killed, but some had been taken prisoner. When the British soldiers retreated after the battle they had to leave many of their wounded in the hands of the Germans.

After three days at war the 93rd had lost 480 soldiers, including those who were killed or wounded on 24 August, almost half of those who had come to France.

Wednesday 26 August began just like the Tuesday had ended with the battalion marching to the south. Before the soldiers left the factory where they had rested, they were given breakfast at four o'clock. Three men shared one tin of meat and they boiled water for tea over small fires. They prepared their rifles and then they were off. They were told that the German cavalry was in the town. Their Brigade was the last unit to leave Le Cateau. The 93rd were at the head of the Brigade. They left the road, which was full of transport wagons, and continued over the fields in a spread-out formation that would avoid several soldiers being hit by one artillery grenade.

The 93rd passed soldiers from other units, who had dug themselves in, made breakfast and prepared to meet the German attack. The soldiers had spent the night out in the fields, lying on corn sheaves in hastily dug holes. The line of defence was on the slope of a ridge south of Le Cateau. James Jack, an officer at the staff of the 19th Brigade, where the 93rd was one of the battalions, saw how difficult it was for the soldiers to build good defences. He wrote that "they were entrenching as well as they could with their wretched little tools, augmented by some village picks and spades."

The 19th Brigade halted by the road a mile or so southwest of the town and waited for orders. A wagon came with water so the soldiers could fill their flasks, but the flow from the tap was so slow that not all of them got any.

Around nine o'clock the 93rd were ordered to go back a short distance, closer to Le Cateau. They were to be prepared to

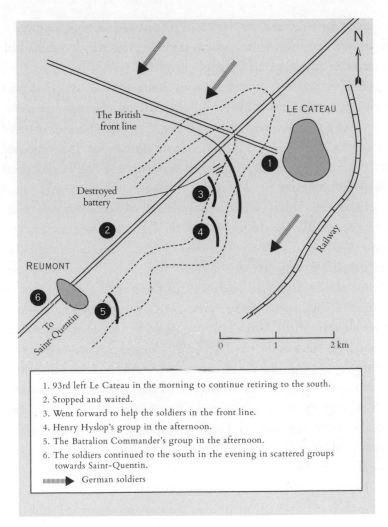

N

The British front line

LE CATEAU

Destroyed battery

REUMONT

To Saint-Quentin

Railway

0   1   2 km

1. 93rd left Le Cateau in the morning to continue retiring to the south.
2. Stopped and waited.
3. Went forward to help the soldiers in the front line.
4. Henry Hyslop's group in the afternoon.
5. The Battalion Commander's group in the afternoon.
6. The soldiers continued to the south in the evening in scattered groups towards Saint-Quentin.

German soldiers

In the battle of Le Cateau on 26 August, the 93rd lost almost half of the soldiers who had come to Boulogne a few weeks earlier.

support the soldiers that they had just passed on the slope, who faced the direction from where the German attack came. The soldiers in the 93rd were still behind the top of the ridge and there they were again told to wait. Soldiers from the transport brought ammunition. This was when the first German grenades fell among them. There was no protection. The Scots were told to dig in, but Henry Hyslop, who commanded B Company, wrote that "beyond keeping the men occupied I don't think their digging did much good."

Next they were ordered to walk on in the same direction, over the top of the ridge. Henry Hyslop could not understand why they were to move up to the frontline. Grenades exploded on the ridge. An artillery battery that stood there had been almost totally destroyed and most of the gunners were killed or wounded. But so far there came no German infantry soldiers. So why should the Scots risk going there, where there was no protection, he wondered. The order seemed to have been given by someone who did not know what was happening. But they must obey orders. Henry Hyslop conferred with the commander of C Company. They agreed to split their companies, taking into account how their platoons were positioned on the ridge. Henry Hyslop advanced with two platoons from his own company and two platoons from C Company.

He wrote: "No sooner did we stand up to advance than the German guns opened on us and gave us absolute hell, the fire seemed to come from all directions..." He also wrote that he was proud to lead men who walked on through the explosions.

Charles Ditcham, who was in Henry Hyslop's company later said in an interview:

"You were put in a corn field and you were told dig yourself in, well, quite frankly I don't know if you have seen what an entrenchment tool looks like in the army... This is how you had to dig yourself in. You might as well have been a rabbit because you could not dig anything."

"You made a bit of a hole in the ground with your entrenching tool and then you took up a position and then the party started and when I mean the party started the hun came along – in his hordes. This is what made me realize what war was about ...[They] came in their hordes and we just shot them down and they still kept coming. There was sufficient of them to shove us out of the field eventually."

The commander of C Company advanced to reinforce the frontline with two platoons from his own company and two platoons from Henry Hyslop's B Company. Their route was even more exposed. Henry Hyslop saw them walk past the demolished artillery pieces: "We never saw them again."

At midday the soldiers from the forward line of holes began to retire, towards the soldiers of the 93rd. German soldiers were seen advancing in the valley on the British soldiers right side, to the east. No British units were there. Henry Hyslop's group fired at the Germans as they left the houses of Le Cateau and succeeded in stopping them, but new German troops came and found protection behind a railway bank. The 93rd's machine guns, which were out on the right also fired, but they were immediately hit by shells. The soldiers were killed or wounded and the weapons were destroyed.

In the afternoon the British commanders decided that it was time for the entire force to retreat. The soldiers in the 93rd noticed that there were no longer any British troops on their left. At the same time more German soldiers came into the valley, to their right. The Scots were fired on from straight ahead, from the sides and even from behind. They realized that they risked being surrounded and decided to also retire. There were two groups, with Henry Hyslop leading one and the commander of the battalion leading the other. When Henry Hyslop walked back he helped carry the lieutenant who had been commanding the machine guns. He was wounded in several places. They left him in the next village, Reumont, where the church was a dressing station. Henry Hyslop wanted to launch an attack at the Germans in the valley to the east, but the commander of another battalion instead ordered him to form a rear-guard and protect a mixed group who walked to the rear, to the south.

In the afternoon of 26 August the commander of the 19th Brigade ordered James Jack to go out and look for soldiers who could form up to protect the rest of the brigade and other brigades when they retired. James Jack had to do this on his own as the commander had no soldiers in reserve and because the situation was so confused that he could not issue a clear order.

James Jack's groom was wounded and the horses had disappeared so he went out on foot, back towards Le Cateau to find a unit. First he met a battalion, the commander of which just said that he had orders to retire and he refused to turn around. Then he met the commander of the 93rd who came marching with his group. James Jack explained the situation and the commander ordered:

"93rd, about turn!"

They turned around and went back into the fighting "...

the movement being executed on the spot with almost parade exactitude," James Jack wrote.

Both Adam McLachlan and Frank Collier wrote briefly about 26 August. Frank Collier just wrote that the Argylls made a 200 yards attack but that they had to halt as a unit to their right retired, which made it possible for German soldiers to fire at them not only from straight ahead but also sideways. Together with some other soldiers he then managed to get a lift to the south with some transport wagons. Adam McLachlan wrote about an "awful battle for our lives" and a "hellish slaughter". In the afternoon they were forced to retire "with hundreds killed, wounded [or] prisoners."

Another soldier in the battalion, J. Stevenson, kept a diary in a small note pad. It is now kept under glass in the museum of the Argyll and Sutherland Highlanders in Stirling. On 26 August he wrote:

"Sudden call to arms. Germans advancing. Big battle in progress. I am writing this at the side of the road. I thank the Lord I am alive to write this ...when we advanced towards the Germans we were falling like sheep. What a sight, shells bursting everywhere. I cannot write anymore about it, the sight will remain with me till I die..."

Charles Ditcham, who was not allowed to carry a rifle, was told to go back. There he met another drummer. Together they carried a badly wounded soldier, whom they knew, to a dressing station in a church, probably the church in Reumont.

"[I had] the shock of my life, all the badly wounded, the stretcher cases and the walking cases they were all there ...the church was full of them."

After they had got out of the fighting the British soldiers resumed their big retreat to the south. Arthur Conan Doyle, author of the books about Sherlock Holmes, wrote in a book that was published in 1916 that there was thunder and flashing as the soldiers walked or dragged themselves through the darkness. But it was not grenades, it was a thunderstorm and the soldiers could wet their lips from the rain.

Charles Ditcham reported that he met a soldier who had driven an ammunition wagon. He had abandoned the wagon and was now walking back with his Clydesdale horses. He lifted Charles Ditcham onto the back of one of the horses and there he sat, half asleep until they came to the town of Saint-Quentin the next morning, some 20 miles south of Le Cateau.

Groups of soldiers from the 93rd came there in the small hours of Thursday 27 August. Along the way they had left many wagons with ammunition, water and other supplies. Among the lost wagons was the officers' mess wagon they had bought in Boulogne. Not that this was so important on a day like this, but Henry Hyslop still recorded it in his diary. It shows what pressure they were under when they stumbled to the south, away from the Germans: "...as [the Mess cart] was hurrying away on a crowded road it upset in a ditch, and there was nothing for Sgt Coyle to do but leave it and its store of whisky and get away with the horse."

The soldiers of the 93rd were not allowed to enter Saint-Quentin so they lay down at the roadside. There they slept.

 ALBERT

Towards Paris

When Albert Schmidt's regiment IR133 had come over on the western side of the river Meuse on 27 August, they marched together with their army corps to the south and forced the French forces to retire. Johannes Niemann has described several fights in which they took part. One day they were fighting Zouaves, who were soldiers from the French colonies in northern Africa. After the fight many dead soldiers could be seen lying in the field, dressed in their red, white and blue uniforms. On another occasion the German soldiers were hit by bullets, but they could not see the French soldiers. Finally the Germans saw that the French were hiding in fruit trees. The Germans fired at the trees with their machine guns and dead French soldiers fell down from the branches. The reason why they had been able to hide was that they belonged to a unit which wore grey uniform trousers, instead of the usual red trousers. This was not a major confrontation. Still the IR133 reported that 45 soldiers had been killed and 92 wounded.

They kept marching to the south and the regiment crossed the river Aisne. One evening their marching route was crossed by a French column. Albert Schmidt's battalion attacked the French soldiers. This was very difficult in the darkness and the battalion was praised by the brigade commander the next day. Again many German soldiers were wounded, among them the commander of Albert Schmidt's company who lost a leg.

The next day, 2 September, Albert Schmidt's battalion

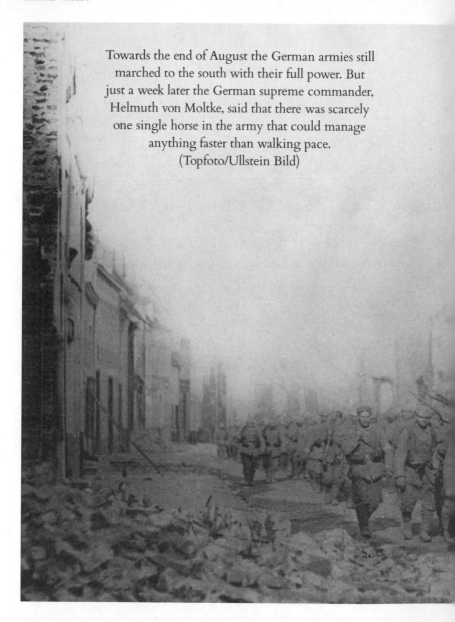

Towards the end of August the German armies still
marched to the south with their full power. But
just a week later the German supreme commander,
Helmuth von Moltke, said that there was scarcely
one single horse in the army that could manage
anything faster than walking pace.
(Topfoto/Ullstein Bild)

were out clearing the battlefield. The other two battalions of the regiment were attacked and formed up to capture a village where French soldiers had built their defence. In this fight Albert Schmidt's football club mate Alfred Lippold was praised for shooting with the machine gun despite French shells exploding all around them. He was not a machine-gunner, but when many gunners and their helpers were killed or wounded other soldiers took their places. This was one of the actions, which were mentioned when Alfred Lippold was later recommended for the Iron Cross, Second Class. When the regiment reported its casualties on 3 September, 54 soldiers were killed, 136 wounded and 33 were missing.

Later the regiment came to the town of Châlons-sur-Marne, where they marched in without fighting. They were led by the colours and the regimental band played. The soldiers had a rest day and they slept in very good billets. Châlons-sur-Marne with 25,000 inhabitants was capital of the departement of Marne and it was the largest town that the soldiers had seen since they entered France. Most shops were closed but a barber in the square was open and did good business.

This was 4 September, the 34th day of the war. According to the plan they had another eight days to force France to capitulate and it was to be achieved, also according to the plan, in a major battle. The whole German force was on the eastern side of Paris. The German supreme commander, Helmuth von Moltke, admitted that the enemy had managed to escape being surrounded. To force the deciding battle he ordered the First Army and the Second Army to stay where they were while the Third Army, where Albert Schmidt's IR133 was one of the regiments, was to press ahead on their eastern side towards the river Seine. The rest of the German force in France was to head southeast, towards the French border with Germany in order to open way for the German forces that were at the border. In this way the German armies could be in position to surround the French and British forces.

That same day Helmuth von Moltke received a visitor who noted that the commander was not at all in a victory mood but rather grave and low-spirited. He confirmed that German soldiers were some 30 miles from Paris, but he added that in all the armies there was scarcely one single horse that could manage anything faster than walking pace.

"We must not allow ourselves to be fooled," Helmuth von Moltke said. "We have been successful, but we have not yet prevailed. When one is opposed by an army of millions, the victor takes prisoners. Where are our prisoners?"

"Also the comparatively small number of captured artillery pieces tells me that that the French have retreated in a planned and orderly fashion. What is most difficult is still to come!"

The soldiers in IR133 resumed their march after the rest and they now went south of the river Marne. The regiment was ordered to attack a French unit at five o'clock one morning west of the town of Vitry-le-François. It is some 120 miles east of Paris. The attack started well and the Germans advanced. But after a few hours they were stopped by French artillery shells. The soldiers could neither advance nor go back. They had to stay where they were all day and those who carried spades dug holes for protection as best they could. It was a hot day and shells exploded among the German soldiers.

The accounts of what happened next differ. Johannes Niemann wrote that they planned to resume their attack in the evening when the French artillery fire seemed to subside. But a unit on their left side could not join the advance so the IR133 could not move forward. Another officer, Hugo Klemm, wrote that his battalion attacked and that the French soldiers were taken by surprise and fled. But the German artillery, which was supposed to fire shells in front of their own infantry either aimed badly or did not know how far the German soldiers had advanced. So the German shells hit their own soldiers. They were also hit by French shells. That is why the attack stopped. Whichever of these stories is true, many Germans had been killed or wounded during the day. When it became dark all the unharmed soldiers had to help carrying the wounded to the dressing station.

One of the wounded soldiers was Alfred Lippold, the football player from Schedewitz. He held out when the shells exploded around him. This was also mentioned when he was recommended for a medal. It was in this fight that he was badly wounded in the leg.

After this unsuccessful attack the XIXth Army Corps, where IR133 was one of eight regiments, made a new attempt. Johannes Niemann wrote that the German soldiers advanced up to where the French artillery guns were positioned. It looked like a breakthrough.

"The French had already been ordered to retreat, we were told later. But the Army command unfortunately did not know this," Johannes Niemann wrote.

Suddenly, when they were on their way forward, the German soldiers heard the signal to retreat. The bugler who blew the signal might have been Albert Schmidt. The Germans broke off their attack. This was as far south as the IR133 reached. It was around nine o'clock in the evening of 10 September. They were ordered to march to the north, but they did not get on their way until next morning, before sunrise.

They must have been tired. A German account of the advance of the Third Army through Belgium and France sums up the first 26 days (24 days for IR133) up to the point where they could not get further south. During 19 of these days the army had been fighting and the soldiers had had only one rest day. A German officer and company commander in the First Army wrote about their trials. He had orders to use all means to make the soldiers keep up the pace when they pursued the French and the British to the south. "Tell them that sweat saves blood," his battalion commander said. The soldiers marched on, some with fleshy sores on their feet. They could stand the pain when they marched towards victory, but it must have been worse when they were ordered to turn back and march past villages that they had passed earlier in the other direction. Officers swore and one colonel wept. It probably did not help much that they explained to the troops that they retreated to regroup in order to hit a new enemy that came from Paris. The soldiers must have understood that they were retreating.

✪ JIMMY ✪

"Rats in a trap"

The British retreat from the Belgian border to near Paris was difficult and dangerous, but it still seems to have been rather orderly. This is the impression I have got after reading the 93rd's war diary. But for the soldiers the retreat must have been confusing or even chaotic.

The drummer Charles Ditcham told about it long after the war: "According to history today it was an orderly retreat, well, as one who took part in the orderly retreat I don't think it was very orderly."

The soldiers also had to make the long march with not enough rest or food. One of the soldiers, Adam McLachlan in A Company wrote in his account of the war: "We were done to the world, we seemed to be like rats in a trap."

He wrote that after they had reached Saint-Quentin on Thursday morning 27 August. It was better the next day: "We got a chance to get a complete refresher and some food, the first for days." But then came days with new painful marches. On some days they were soaked by rain, on other days they marched under a scorching sun. Their glengarry caps did not give them much protection. Instead they protected their heads with turnip leaves that grew in the fields or they took branches from the trees for shade. They walked through orchards and picked the fruit although it was not ripe. They searched for food in deserted villages but they did not find much. Frank Collier in A Company cooked together with a comrade and they shared the food. They managed to catch an old hen, which they cooked. He also wrote that one of the officers found a wine cellar where there was wine, rum and brandy. The officer told the soldiers to half fill their flasks and top them up with water. Then they resumed their march to the south, many of them with sore feet. After marching the whole day they slept under their waterproof sheets, sometimes in a damp field.

The battalion was split into several groups. The officers tried to unite the groups but they got neither orders nor directions or they were sent the wrong way. Some groups were ordered to get on trains. Henry Hyslop was in command of a group with some 200 men. They squeezed into a train in Saint-Quentin. On the next track was a train loaded with supplies and they were told to help themselves to food, "...this we did, very liberally." The train set off, but when it came to the station where they were to get off it did not stop long enough. Several officers and many men were stuck on the train "...and worst of all, with our stock of food from the supply train." Another group was put on a train that ended up in Le Mans, nearly 200 miles away, on the other side of Paris.

The Germans watched the British retreat. The soldiers saw aeroplanes and balloons and they saw German horsemen who followed them at a distance and who sometimes fired shells at the marching columns. The 19th Brigade, where the 93rd was one of four battalions, was sometimes the rear-guard. On several occasions they formed up for defence and dug themselves in. But the Germans never attacked in force.

The rearguard was also responsible for forcing worn out soldiers, who had lost touch with their units, to march on. The soldiers did this with fixed bayonets, Frank Collier wrote. The general in command of the brigade had ordered the commander of the 93rd to shoot soldiers who refused to keep on walking. But in the accounts that I have studied I have not found any information that this actually happened.

After a painful and hot march on Thursday 3 September Henry Hyslop wrote: "We are now within 20 miles of Paris." On the following Saturday, 5 September, the last group of soldiers rejoined the battalion. There were supplies also. The soldiers could wash and they were given their first rations of tobacco. Frank Collier used paper from one of his letters to roll cigarettes. The 93rd had reached a turning point in the war.

In the trenches

A retreat they could not understand

Eleventh September dawned with dull autumn weather. Albert Schmidt and the other soldiers in IR133 were more or less due east from Paris, where they had broken off their attack against the French just as they were about to break through. From there they started their march toward the north. In the afternoon it started to rain. The rolling field kitchens got stuck in the congestion among the retreating units on the road and could not keep up with the soldiers. Most of them did not understand why they retreated. Johannes Niemann wrote that they grumbled, saying: "We did our bit."

I would like to stop here to ask a few difficult questions: Does Johannes Niemann's account ring true? Can we believe that the soldiers were complaining that they found themselves marching on a road instead of running in a field where enemy soldiers shot at them with rifles and guns? Or were the Germans instead relieved because they were spared from attacking? Were they actually grateful because they had come through yet another fight without being killed or wounded?

I cannot put myself in their place. But I have got the impression that the soldiers at this time had learnt much about living in the war and surviving. They must have known what was less dangerous and what was more dangerous. With this knowledge they would rather have been on the road than in the field. On the other hand, neither can I put myself in their place when they went to war. There are accounts of soldiers who looked forward to the fighting and if one chooses not to believe these accounts there are pictures to back them up.

The Scottish drummer Charles Ditcham has described the difference between advancing and retiring:

"As long as you were going forward and pushing the Germans you could go forever. To go the other way, you were depressed forever. That was my feeling. Your whole morale was down in your boots."

So what are the answers to the questions? I think the answers go both ways. Some soldiers must have been relieved to be on the road. Possibly these soldiers were veterans, who had been with the regiment since August. Others, perhaps newcomers who were still eager to kill enemy soldiers, might rather have carried on the attack. Perhaps they felt their pride had been dented when they were forced to break off the attack when it was going well. And the answer could be even more complicated. Perhaps there were soldiers who wished they had been allowed to stay in the field, where they had the upper hand and where they were on verge of achieving what the officers had talked about all autumn, but who were at the same time happy to be safe for the moment.

Anyway they were right in that the IR133 had not been beaten, although 643 soldiers were reported dead, wounded or missing during the days 6–11 September. That is at least one fifth of the regiment. The second battalion, with just over 1,000 men according to the organizational tables, had shrunk to just one company. But these terrible losses were not the reason why they had been ordered to retreat. The reason was that other German forces had been attacked and forced to retreat in what in the history books is known as the Battle of the Marne.

When the German Third Army reached the end of their advance to the south it was about 125 miles east of Paris. To the west of the Third Army was the Second Army and to the west of the Second Army was the First Army. This army was close to Paris. There were no German forces to the west of the First Army.

France had assembled a new army near Paris. This army attacked the western side of the German First Army. The attack had to be made without delay while the German First Army was not yet so well protected on its western side. The French needed to quickly bring up reinforcements. Thus hundreds of taxicabs were stopped in the streets of Paris. The passengers were ordered out of the cars and the drivers were ordered to pick up soldiers and drive them to the front. This French attack was not in itself decisive, but it forced the German First Army to turn more to the west. This weakened the front to the south, which opened a gap between the First and Second Army. French and British forces advanced into this gap.

After a few days the German Second Army had to retreat to the north and when they did so the First and Third Armies had to retreat. This was why Albert Schmidt's regiment IR133 had to break off their attack and march to the north.

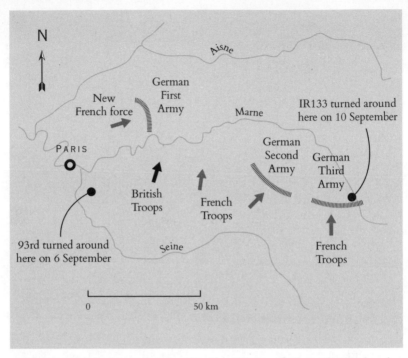

The war reached a turning point when Jimmy Coyle in the 93rd and Albert Schmidt in IR133 were east of Paris. The German First Army was forced to turn at a new French force. When this happened French and British soldiers could attack the German First Army and Second Army from the side. They were made to retire. IR133, as part of the Third Army, was also forced to turn around.

When the regiment crossed the river Marne, back to the northern bank, engineers stood ready at the bridge. French soldiers tried to follow the Germans across but then the bridge was blown up. The Saxons marched to the north along the river. After some 35 miles they started digging themselves in, but they were sent further north. The soldiers were angry when they set off, Johannes Niemann wrote. A thunderstorm raged above their heads. "Only those who were there can understand how we felt."

They halted at last near the town of Moumelon-le-Grand, which they had passed on their way south. They stayed there for almost three weeks. This became their first experience of trench warfare.

The trenches were simple compared with those that were built later, but the soldiers could improve them with planks and branches. Their position was on a hill at the edge of a wood. In front of them, to the south, was a valley with a farm and a hill. There was a windmill on the hill.

The French had occupied the farm and the hill, but IR133 took the hill. The regiment reported 230 lost soldiers (killed, wounded or missing) on 19 September. On 26 September the regiment lost 55 soldiers and on 27 September another 36. One of the company commanders was among the killed. On 28 September Albert Schmidt took part in an attack and got into a French trench. For this he was awarded the Iron Cross, Second Class.

The IR133 remained in this position until 4 October. Then the regiment, together with the XIXth Corps was transferred from the Third Army to the Sixth Army. This army was moved from Lorraine to the area along the border between France and Belgium, near the Channel coast. IR133 set off to the west, marching and by train. This was part of what came to be called the race to the sea, when both sides tried to attack the enemy from the west or even get around the enemy line and attack from behind. The Germans also tried to capture the harbours at the Channel coast, where the British landed their supplies and reinforcements. The British then moved their forces there, to defend the harbours. On 11 October the IR133 was near Lille, the important industrial centre and railway hub in northern France. The XIXth Corps took Lille before the IR133 could join the fighting.

The Corps' next task was to fight the British west of Lille. What was most important was to prevent the British from moving forces from this area to the area around the medieval town of Ypres in Belgium. The Germans attacked there in order to break through and reach the coast and the harbours. This fight is called The First Battle of Ypres.

⊜ JIMMY ⊜

Turning around

The day after all groups of the 93rd found each other east of Paris they marched to the north. It was 6 September. The French, helped by the British, attacked the Germans and forced them back to the north of the river Marne. Many German units also had to cross the river Aisne. The 93rd was not in the front during these attacks but followed behind and the soldiers saw what had taken place. Frank Collier wrote that black smoke came from a wood where French soldiers had caught the Germans. The French had set fire to the wood and then shot Germans who tried to escape, or killed them with bayonets. Beyond the wood was a field where dead French and German soldiers lay, covered with some straw. Henry Hyslop wrote about a village they passed through. The houses were pillaged and "the roads and empty spaces were almost paved with empty bottles where the Germans had looted the cellars and drunk the wine." Dead men lay in ditches together with dead horses.

A few days later, in another village, soldiers of the 93rd were sent out to bury German soldiers who had been killed by shells. Aidan Liddell, a newly arrived officer, wrote: "Had to collect bits in a waterproof sheet." They also buried dead horses, which was hard work. All the time they were within reach of shells from the German artillery. Soldiers were killed or wounded. Horses were killed as well and several transport wagons were destroyed.

The 93rd stayed in this area near the river Aisne until 5 October. They then marched to the west, mostly during nights when German airmen could not see the marching columns. During the night between 9 and 10 October, the soldiers got on a freight train. Henry Hyslop wrote that the men were herded like cattle and that there was not room for them to lie down.

After 15 hours on the train they came to northern France, near the coast and near the border with Belgium. They came there because the BEF had taken over responsibility for the western end of the front. The British were to co-operate with what was left of the Belgian army and their task was to stop the Germans from reaching the coast.

The 19th Brigade, where the 93rd was one of the battalions, did not belong to one specific unit but was sent here and there, where there was a gap to fill. On 20 October there was such a gap at the village of Le Maisnil, some 10 miles west of Lille. The 93rd got there before dawn on Saturday 21 October. The soldiers were told to build defences directed to the east and the south. The orders were to stop attacks: "...retirement is only to be carried out in case of absolute necessity..."

The 93rd had been in their defences at Le Maisnil for about an hour when the Germans started firing artillery shells at them. After yet another hour German soldiers attacked and they kept attacking while shells were still exploding among the Scots. One shell burst near the wagon carrying ammunition for the machine guns. The horses ran away until the wagon overturned after half a mile. The officer in command of the area was killed.

Units from other battalions came to the front to help. The British kept on firing and they must have hit hundreds of Germans, killing or wounding them. Soldiers in the 93rd were also killed or wounded by bullets or shells. Late in the afternoon they left their holes and walked back. The stretcher-bearers managed to bring 56 wounded soldiers to the transport but many other wounded were left behind in the darkness.

It is difficult to understand how the stretcher-bearers could evacuate so many. They worked in the middle of the fighting. Many stretcher-bearers were decorated for bravery. The 93rd's doctor wrote in 1915 about how he himself on one occasion had helped carry a wounded soldier.

"I gave him morphine and we got him on the stretcher and then started to get him back... It was a terrible business, struggling knee-deep in tenacious mud, walking over slippery planks, with machine-gun bullets hitting the ground and trees and other things all round us ...I never realised until that night what it was to carry a stretcher ...There is no finer body of men in the whole army than the regimental stretcher-bearers."

One of the officers in the 93rd, James Cunningham, wrote

about the terrible decisions that commanders had to make when wounded soldiers were left behind. This happened when they were on their way back from Le Maisnil:

"...one of our men was wounded and we carried him into an empty cottage that we were passing. Putting him on a bed, we saw one round black hole just above his kilt, virtually no blood and obviously very serious. At that moment, Hyslop entered, took one look at the wound and in a most peremptory voice said, 'Get out'. I thought it awful to leave the poor man but the tone of the order brooked no delay and we went. I do not think we were fifty yards down the road when a large German shell took the house at its foundations and put it right across the road. Not one of us would have survived had Hyslop's order not been obeyed instantly."

James Cunningham wrote that his company reassembled in the evening: "I remember standing while the roll was called in the dark, close to a blacksmith's shop and I think we numbered somewhere about 32, having gone into action at full strength i.e. about 230 strong." This casualty figure seems too high, perhaps because some soldiers had lost touch with their company during the fighting. One group of soldiers in the company came back in the small hours. They had been hiding and could not move until it was dark. Both the battalion's war diary and Henry Hyslop's diary (he was the commander of this company) say that the casualties for the whole battalion was "over 200" soldiers, killed, wounded or missing.

The war diary of the 93rd sums up in a few lines what happened at Le Maisnil. Several wounded were left with the Germans. The transport wagons were also left behind. More to be left who could not walk and these fell into German hands. The Germans did not press on so the Battalion marched on to LA BOUTILLERIE to bivouack. Wounded taken over by Ambulances. Transport had also to be abandonned.

Bivouacked in field with 1/MIDDLESEX Regt. Capts URE & SANDEMAN, Lieuts CAMPBELL (I.L.) FAIRLIE, & BLACKLOCK and over 200 men missing. 1 Platoon A Coy (Lord ERSKINE, Lieut) and 1 Platoon D Coy (Lieut AITKEN) still to come in. "A" Coy (less 1 Platoon) took up a covering position, in line with the CAMERONIANS and MIDDLESEX Regt, about 200° to the front.

Lieut AITKEN'S Platoon (D Coy) marched in

Lieut LORD ERSKINE'S Platoon marched in

1 Section "B" Coy came in, having lain in a trench, undiscovered by the Germans, and made good their escape under cover of darkness [Stood to arms]

CAMERONIANS 1/MIDDLESEX and 1/ROYAL WELSH FUSILIERS to hold the

The war diary of the 93rd sums up in a few lines what happened at Le Maisnil. Several wounded were left with the Germans. The transport wagons were also left behind. More than 200 soldiers were missing. This is probably the figure for casualties – soldiers killed, wounded, missing or taken prisoners. Two groups came back later. They had been hiding and slipped away when it was dark.

than 200 soldiers were missing. This is probably the figure for casualties – soldiers killed, wounded, missing and taken prisoner. Two groups came back later. They had been hiding and slipped away when it was dark.

Jimmy Coyle is not mentioned in any of the accounts of the fight at Le Maisnil, but he must have been close to the front with the transport wagons. The battalion headquarters were in a ditch near the front defences. This is where the officer in command of the area was mortally wounded. Shells hit several transport wagons and when the 93rd left Le Maisnil they left all wagons behind. This meant that the 93rd lost its war diary for the second time. The diary for October had to be reconstructed and it was not signed until 17 December.

Two days after the fight at Le Maisnil the battalion had withdrawn a few miles to the west. Then Jimmy Coyle seems to have been nearly hit. The mess wagon stood outside a cottage, which was the battalion's headquarters and soldiers carried food into the cottage. A shell burst nearby and frightened the horse. A soldier stepped forward to take the halter. As he did that he was hit by a splinter from a shell.

JIMMY

Barbed wire

The 93rd received their first coils of barbed wire towards the end of October.

The battalion were in trenches between Armentières (on the British side of the front) and Lille (on the German side) in northern France. This was near the place where they had stopped after they had retreated from Le Maisnil on 21 October. They were responsible for part of the frontline, but their part was much smaller than those held by the other battalions. The reason was there were so few soldiers left in the 93rd, just 200–300, according to an officer in the brigade staff.

Both the British and the Germans now started building

trenches. It was the beginning of a system of ditches that soon stretched from the North Sea to the Swiss border and where much of the war was to be fought during the coming four years. The first trenches were simple compared to those that were built later. The barbed wire entanglements were also simple, but in spite of that German soldiers got caught in them. Adam McLachlan was sent out in the darkness to take down dead Germans who hanged on the loops of wire.

There were not yet any communication trenches between the frontline and the trenches in the second line, nor were there any communication trenches between the fire trenches of each company. When a soldier had to move from one trench to another trench there was a risk that he exposed himself to the German snipers. These had an advantage because their positions were on slightly higher ground than the Scots' positions. The snipers also killed soldiers who showed their heads above the parapet. It was a bullet from a sniper that had killed the commander at Le Maisnil.

Because the British trenches were on lower ground they collected a lot of water and the bottom of the trenches became muddy. The soldiers walked in mud and mud stuck to their clothes and their rifles. Mud got into the barrels of their rifles and they could not be cleaned. Soldiers in the front trench had to take rifles from those who were behind, in reserve.

Life in the trenches was horrid. On top of that the enemy attacked. During two weeks after the fight at Le Maisnil the battalion repulsed two ground attacks. During six of those days German shells exploded around the trenches or behind.

The worst grenades were those with a calibre of 15 centimetres, loaded with high explosive. They made craters big enough for a dozen men. When these grenades exploded there was a column of black smoke. They were called Jack Johnsons, named after a black American heavyweight boxing champion. There are stories about Jack Johnsons that sound plucky or downright happy-go-lucky. But these grenades killed soldiers and tore them to pieces.

Frederick Chandler, a doctor who at this time worked in the 19th Brigade, wrote in a letter:

"I suppose people at home think Jack Johnsons are rather a joke – they are about the most devilish things ever conceived. Their effect on morale and nerve is incalculable. I have seen men weeping when they have got away from them. The shriek of them, the ear-splitting explosion, the awful ruin they create – they are damnable things."

Grenades were a terrible part of the soldiers' everyday life. Doctor Chandler wrote that "one always puts on a nonchalant air to set them an example and prevent any panic and one almost persuades oneself that one doesn't mind." But the grenades were dangerous and frightening. "The men in the trenches and those who have been under heavy shell fire have a terrible look on their faces," the doctor wrote.

The war of 1914–1918 was the first in history when artillery grenades killed more soldiers than illness or bullets. According to a German estimate the artillery killed twice as many soldiers than the infantry during the first year of the war.

The technique to fire grenades with canons (straight on, on a flat trajectory) and howitzers (on a high trajectory, so that grenades hit the ground almost vertically) had been significantly improved, starting at the turn of the century. Methods to handle

The worst German shells were called Jack Johnsons after an
American boxer. Frederick Chandler, the battalion doctor of the
93rd, wrote that they were "about the most devilish things ever
conceived." The picture shows one of his colleagues standing in a
shell hole to show how deep it is.
(Frederick Chandler, Imperial War Museum, HU 128733)

the recoil were important. They meant that the gun did not move so much as it was fired so it could be quickly aimed again for the next grenade.

The French 75 mm piece could fire one grenade every fourth second or even every second second. People who knew the sound of them could distinguish the French 75s from other guns. Horace Smith-Dorrien, commander of the British Second Army corps could do that. When his soldiers retreated from Le Cateau on 26 August he heard intensive artillery fire in the distance. He was worried until the rhythm of the fire told him that it was the French who were firing, not the Germans.

Another development was that the artillery was moved to the back so far away from the front that the gunners could not see where they were aiming. They received instructions from observers who were with the infantry in the frontline. Many observers sent their instructions by wire telephones, but they often lost contact with their batteries because the wires were cut by shell explosions or maybe by soldiers stepping on them. The artillery had fought in this way during the Russo–Japanese war in 1904–1905. The great military powers had been there to learn about this new method of fighting, but traditionalists in the British Army still wanted the artillery to be with the frontline troops. The artillery was positioned in this way at Le Cateau and that was the reason why so many gunners were killed and so many guns were destroyed or lost; for example the battery that was lost near where the 93rd were during the fight.

Both sides in the war fired shells loaded with shrapnel and shells loaded with high explosive. Shrapnel was made from bullets that were spread out when a charge exploded. It was like a

The First World War was the first war when artillery killed more soldiers than bullets or illness. The picture shows the most common British gun, an 18 pounder, in position near Ploegsteert Wood in November 1914. (Imperial War Museum, Q56163)

shot from a giant shotgun. Shrapnel shells were most dangerous when they exploded a couple of yards above the ground. If they burst higher up the bullets were not always dangerous.

These shells were also used to destroy barbed wire entanglements, with limited effect, but they could not hurt soldiers in a dugout. Grenades with high explosive power could be fired by howitzers, for example the German 15 cm howitzers.

These shells hit the ground almost vertically. Sometimes they had detonators which were set to burst with a small delay when the shell had penetrated into the ground. Then they could kill soldiers who had sought protection in a dugout. But in a way shells from howitzers were less dangerous because soldiers could hear them coming which gave them a few moments to seek cover. Shells from canons, however, exploded without warning.

It was the German 15 cm howitzers that launched the Jack Johnsons. The British had similar grenades, and soldiers from both sides have told about what it was like being near bursting high explosives.

One soldier tells that soldiers tried to find brandy to get drunk. They longed to lose their ability to feel. Another wrote that the law of gravity seemed no longer to be in force. Others tell about soldiers who lost their wits. Some tried with their hands to dig for a comrade in a caved-in dugout only to be buried themselves by the next grenade.

The explosions could cut a man down the middle or annihilate a human body. Those who were nearby were then sprayed with scraps of flesh, blood and stomach contents. Victims were sometimes thrown up in the air and parts of their bodies were spread over a big area. It also happened that a soldier was killed without a trace of a scar because the blast had destroyed his lungs or other internal organs.

One British gunner wrote:

"There was no past to remember or future to think about. Only the present. The present agony of waiting, waiting for the shell that was coming to destroy us, waiting to die ...None of us spoke. I shut my eyes, I saw nothing. But I could not shut my ears – I heard everything, the screaming of the shells, the screams of pain, the terrifying explosions, the vicious fragments of iron rushing downwards, biting deeply into the earth all round us."

The soldiers in the 93rd stayed in the trenches for nine days. Those who were not at the front spent the days in simple shelters, dug into the earth. They gave protection against shrapnel but not against a Jack Johnson. Or they were out digging trenches. They spent the nights under their waterproof sheets in fields further back from the front. On 1 November they marched away, but not to rest. They kept on digging.

Soldiers who were not on guard duty or on other duties during the day rested in shelters some way behind the frontline. There they had protection against shrapnel but not against high explosive shells. The picture shows soldiers in the First Battalion of The Cameronians regiment, which was in the same brigade as Jimmy Coyle's 93rd.
(Imperial War Museum, Q51530)

"Rather a forlorn hope"

On the morning of 7 November, the 93rd were again out digging trenches near Armentières in northern France, near the border with Belgium. They were ordered to stop working and instead march a couple of miles to the Belgian village of Ploegsteert. There the soldiers spent the night under their waterproof sheets in a wet field outside the village. Next day, 8 November, they went into Ploegsteert Wood to take over trenches near the eastern edge of the wood. From there the battalion attacked over a field at midnight, Monday 9 November.

What makes this attack stand out is that it does not stand out. It was not exactly a routine job – it is mentioned with 79 words in the official British history of the war and with 67 words in the regimental history – but it was just one of many, many similar attacks.

The 93rd went out into the field with 330 soldiers. Of those 58 did not come back. They were killed or were reported missing. Another 72 soldiers were wounded. Two thirds of the force came back more or less unhurt, but they had not been able to reach any of their goals. Still the battalion received a message of congratulation from John French, supreme commander of the British Expeditionary Force.

When I studied the attack at Ploegsteert Wood, I found much that I do not understand. How could commanders give orders that would cause so much suffering to reach a gain that was so small besides being so uncertain? One can argue that the

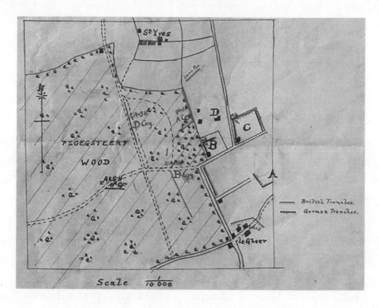

This map of the field where the battalion attacked in the evening of 9 November is in the war diary of the 93rd. D was a house in the field. B and C were the German positions that the 93rd was ordered to attack. The British trenches were in the wood.

war was like that. Soldiers were spent all the time in what was called the daily wastage, which meant that soldiers were killed even when they did not take part in a fight. Perhaps they were just out digging or went to get food. But even if one accepts this it is impossible to understand how commanders could use their best soldiers so carelessly.

As the autumn went by the battalions at the front lost

experienced soldiers. At the same time the number of trained reservists who could be sent to the front from the regiments back home diminished. Around New Year there were hardly any left. In December the supreme commander John French complained to the war department about the new soldiers who came to France. He said they neither could, nor wanted, to fight. They were over 50 years old and they had not fired live ammunition since the war in South Africa ten years earlier. Therefore one would have expected the commanders to save their best soldiers for the most important fights. Still they sent the 93rd across the field at Ploegsteert Wood.

To follow my story I now ask the reader to take time to study the maps on the next page. They will help explain how the soldiers lived and fought during the following days. They are based on the map in the battalion war diary (opposite) and the accounts of soldiers who took part.

The companies that went into the Ploegsteert Wood were A, B and half of D. The machine guns were on loan to another battalion. C Company and half of D Company were also away on loan to help retake a village nearby.

The 93rd left the village of Ploegsteert around four o'clock in the afternoon of 8 November. When the soldiers reached the wood it was getting dark. The wood was dense so they had to keep to the track, which was trodden by many feet down to the Flanders mud. Horses could not walk there nor could anything on wheels pass by. The soldiers walked in single file. They slipped and splashed through the mud. The distance from the village through the wood is only about two miles but it took them two hours to get to their positions.

Attack at Ploegsteert Wood

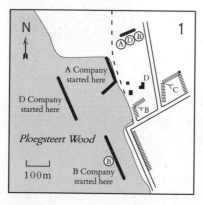

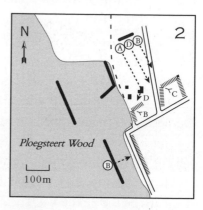

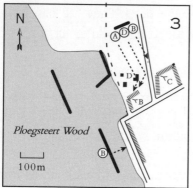

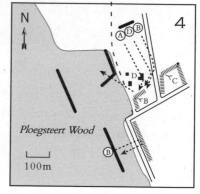

— British trenches	Ⓐ Ⓑ Ⓓ These companies took part in the attack.
▥ German trenches	B C German positions marked on the British map (page 112).
⊰ Machine gun	D Houses in the field.

The ditches in the field at Ploegsteert Wood held water to the rims in December 2012. This is where the soldiers of the 93rd crouched in shallow trenches on 9 November before they set out to conquer the German trenches. These were among the trees at the far, southern, end of the field. (Pehr Thermaenius)

1. The main force formed up in another battalion's trench to attack from the north. Only half of B Company stayed in its trench, from where they were to make a feint attack.

2. A Company first advanced to the house D, then towards the trench B. A shell had set fire to the house. The fire illuminated the field. D Company came near the trench C and were ordered to charge. In that moment the company commander was hit and fell. The half of B Company made their feint attack across the road.

3. The soldiers in D Company lost their direction and got mixed up with A Company. Together they charged at B, but had to give up when German soldiers fired from C.

4. The officer of B Company tried to assemble the soldiers for a new attack against B. German soldiers in trenches B and C fired at them. The Scots gave up and retired to A Company's trench. B Company broke off their feint attack and went back to their trench.

Henry Hyslop saw that soldiers walked barefoot. He wrote that they had lost their boots in the mud. But Frank Collier wrote that many walked in their socks to avoid just that, to avoid losing their boots.

The battalion took over the trenches in the small hours on Monday 9 November. These trenches had been dug hastily a few days earlier and they were bad, even compared to what existed so early in the war. They were shallow and muddy, there was nowhere to cook and there was no water for washing. Drinking water had to be carried from Ploegsteert along the muddy track. The soldiers ate their emergency rations cold and dry.

British units had earlier been driven out of trenches in front of where the 93rd now were and counterattacks had failed. Frank Collier described what they saw when it dawned.

"There were many dead (British and German) lying in front and behind us. We took rifles off our dead in case of emergency and my rifle breaking down owing to mud in the breech. I took one belonging to a member of the Hants Regiment."

The battalion's trenches were near the eastern edge of the wood. The Germans were in trenches in a field close to the wood and behind a road that runs along the edge of the wood.

The Scots had to improve the trenches. Frank Collier wrote that they dug them three feet deep, so there could not have been room for the soldiers to stand or even sit, just lie in their shallow ditch in the November mud. Artillery grenades exploded all around them. "We had to keep well into earth as we were in greater danger of annihilation from British shell fire than the Germans," Frank Collier wrote. The battalion war diary says one officer was wounded by a British shell. James Cunningham, one of the officers, also wrote that one officer in B Company was killed by a British shell.

The war diary says that the soldiers "spent a quiet morning in the trenches." It does not mention that they were tired, hungry, thirsty, wet, cold, smeared with mud, surrounded by human corpses and that at any time they risked being killed by shrapnel or by bullets from the German trenches in the field.

I visited this field in December 2012. The ground was wet. Water stood in puddles in the grass and in the furrows in the next field. The ditches were full of water that seemed to have nowhere to go. The earth was more like mud than like earth and it stuck to my rubber boots. I jumped over a ditch to get into the wood. The grass on the opposite side looked stable, but when my foot landed on it, it gave way and my foot slid into the ditch. There was only a thin layer of grassy turf with the mud laying underneath, waiting. I do not pretend that I could understand, only perhaps get an idea of what it was like for the soldiers of the 93rd to lie in their newly dug ditches and then make the attack over the field, churned up by shellfire.

In the afternoon of 8 November the battalion had been warned that they would be ordered to make an attack to retake the German trenches across the field. This was confirmed at midday on 9 November. But the soldiers were not told. Frank Collier wrote that it was not until late in the evening that he heard a rumour that something was on. He does not seem to have known for sure until just before it was time to go out.

The plan was for the battalion to attack the German trenches just before midnight. They were to attack not straight ahead but from the side, from the north. But half of B Company was to make a feint attack straight ahead to make it look like the whole attack was coming from that direction.

The commanders must have realized that this would be a very dangerous attack and that many of the men who went into the field would be either killed or wounded. It is also clear that the officers realized that they would probably not be able to drive the German soldiers out of their trenches. Henry Hyslop, who at this time was the battalion's second in command, wrote:

"Two attacks to retake these trenches had failed, and the 93rd are to have another try to-night on what seems rather a forlorn hope. The Germans have greatly improved their position, strongly wired it and brought up machine-guns; and we are not at all certain where their trenches are actually placed."

Still the soldiers were sent into the field to attack.

Frank Collier and his comrades in A Company were taken by their company commander to their starting point, which was a trench held by another British battalion. They lost their way in the wood and reached their starting trench at the last minute, so they had not time to take their direction properly before it was time to set off. The starting signal was three salvoes from the British artillery, which had been firing at the German trenches for half an hour. The starting point for the attack was at the northern end of the field. A Company was first to attack some houses in the field and then attack the German trenches marked B on the map in the war diary. To the left of A Company, to the east, D Company was to attack the German trench that is marked with C on the map. The half of B Company, that was not making the feint attack, was to go on the extreme left side of the attack, the eastern side, to help D Company.

A Company reached the house (marked D on the map) and took one German soldier prisoner. They then continued toward the trench B. Then things went wrong. A British shell had set the house on fire. The fire lit up the field so that the Germans saw the Scots coming and could fire at them. Still D Company managed to come near their objective. The company commander gave the order "Charge!" Immediately after that he was hit and fell.

When the soldiers in D Company lost their leader they lost their direction and moved too much to the right so that they got mixed up with the soldiers in A Company. Together these soldiers tried to attack A Company's objective (B on the map). They managed to cut the barbed wire and get through. But because the German soldiers in the trench marked C were not attacked they could fire from the side at the Scots at the B trench. There came bullets from rifles and from a machine gun at the corner of the C trench. Some Scots, Frank Collier was one of them, managed to enter the German trench marked B "...but with enfilade machine-gun fire we were forced to relinquish our prize so dearly bought," he wrote. So the Scots had to withdraw and leave many comrades behind, among them Frank Collier's company commander. He was wounded in the German trench, he was taken prisoner and brought to a field hospital, but he died there a week later.

Another officer, in command of the half of B Company, then took charge of all the Scots and made a new attempt to take the trench marked B. They were hit by bullets from rifles and machine-guns in both the B and C trenches, where new German soldiers had come. So the Scots had to give up again. They withdrew to the trench where A Company had spent the day.

Meanwhile the other half of B Company, that was to make the feint attack straight ahead, had reached the edge of the wood. When they got there they saw that the artillery had damaged a hedge, which earlier had been impossible to get through. They tried to attack the German trench through the gaps in the hedge, but the fire from the defenders was too powerful so the Scots had to break off their attack. Then the Germans made a counterattack, which the Scots managed to fend off. After that they were ordered to withdraw.

It was now three o'clock at night on 10 November. The soldiers of the 93rd lay in the trenches they had taken over 24 hours earlier. Frank Collier wrote that they had been forced to leave many wounded behind out in the field "...and till next morning we heard the groans and cries of the men who were not yet but nearly dead."

The battalion war diary confirms his account:

"The wounded had been brought back to the trenches originally held by the battalion, and now carried further back. A number could however not be found."

Early in the morning of 10 November the soldiers were ordered to go back into the wood. Frank Collier wrote that they walked with their bayonets still fixed to their rifles.

"We were unable to detach them from our rifles owing to the fact of their being covered with mud and blood. We were also covered likewise from head to foot. When we saw each other in full daylight we were hardly recognizable. Our faces were white under the mud and our eyes were bloodshot and staring."

The battalion spent the following days in the wood. Some soldiers were sent back to the front, others were digging trenches.

They walked out of the wood on Friday 13 November and continued to the village of Ploegsteert where they had breakfast. It was potatoes and Maconochie – tinned meat stew. The war diary notes that this was the first time the soldiers had hot food since they entered the wood on Sunday night.

Frank Collier wrote that they formed up in a field.

"When roll was called the whole regiment numbered 101."

I have no reason to doubt Frank Collier's account, but I would like to point out that the war diary and the regimental history have other figures. Of these two the regimental history seems to be the most reliable because it was written in peace and quiet after the war when there was time to check the figures.

The regimental history says that 330 soldiers took part in the attack. Fifty-eight were killed or were missing and 72 were wounded, all together 130 lost soldiers. So there should have been 200 soldiers present when the roll was called. I cannot say why there is a difference of 99 soldiers between Frank Collier's account and the regimental history. The explanation might be that soldiers, who had lost contact with the battalion during the fighting or later in the wood, had not yet returned when the 93rd left the wood on Friday.

In the 93rd were also C Company and half of D Company that were not with the battalion in the wood. Frank Collier wrote that C Company at this time had shrunk to 16 soldiers. D Company had probably lost at least half of its soldiers and shrunk to about 100 men, of whom 50 were not in the attack on 9 November. The machine guns, with perhaps 20 soldiers, were somewhere else with another battalion. So at least about 90 soldiers should be added to the force that came out of the wood.

To sum it up, the strength of the battalion on 13 November was about 300 soldiers (according to the regimental history) or about 200 soldiers (according to Frank Collier).

Both these figures show that the 93rd had had terrible losses. The battalion came to France with about 1,000 soldiers. Up to 9 November 343 new soldiers had come from home. Of these about 1,343 soldiers there remained 300 or 200. If I use the figure from the regimental history the loss was just over 1,000 (not taking into account that some of the soldiers from home might have been wounded soldiers who had recovered and now returned to the battalion). Since the battalion came to Boulogne on 11 August it had, in 95 days, lost approximately the same number of soldiers that had gone ashore.

This loss was more than twice as big as the calculated loss for an infantry battalion, according to the pre-war edition of the handbook, *Field Service Manual*: "...44 per cent, for the first six months, or 80 per cent, during the first year of a war."

The commanders higher up had evidently got used to losses of this magnitude. If they had been the least surprised or grieved by so much killing and suffering they would probably have chosen other words when they wrote to the 93rd after the attack. They would probably not have written:

"Congratulations on your excellent work last night. With a little luck you would have achieved a great success."

But that was the message to the soldiers from the staff of the general who ordered the attack. Bad luck!

⬡ ALBERT ⬡

Quiet, but still dangerous

In the middle of October the XIXth German Army corps moved to the west from Lille. The corps stayed there and fought against the British during the coming months.

To begin with the fighting was intense, especially around the village of Frelinghien, Johannes Niemann wrote in his book. It was there, in the flat fields, that Saxons and Scots met in No Man's Land at Christmas.

The second battalion of IR133, which was not Albert Schmidt's battalion, took part in a fight for the brewery in Frelinghien on 26 October. The British were forced to leave the brewery. The building had thick walls that gave protection and from the top there was a good view over the trenches that ran to the south across the flat landscape. Erich von Falkenhayn, the supreme commander of the German forces climbed to the top of the brewery in November to study the front where he prepared a major attack.

The second battalion of IR133 then fought in the trenches on the edge of Ploegsteert Wood. This was not far from where the 93rd, Jimmy Coyle's battalion, attacked on 9 November.

Towards the end of October there was less fighting in IR133's area. It was even an area where the Germans sent units that needed a rest. Still, soldiers in the regiment were killed or wounded during 43 of the 65 days that remained until the truce in the evening of 24 December. During these 65 days 26 soldiers were killed, 171 were wounded and nine were reported missing.

German and British soldiers often stood in mud and could not dry their feet. In one British battalion the soldiers smeared their feet with leftover grease that the cooks collected and sent to the front trenches. The picture shows German soldiers during the winter 1914–1915.
(Imperial War Museum, Q63538)

At this time the regiment's strength was about 2,700 men, so the loss was seven per cent. Almost one per cent of the soldiers were killed. This happened while there was no fighting worth mentioning going on.

The regiment fought not only against the British but also against the enemies of all soldiers: the water, the mud and the diseases that prospered in the miserable trenches. Colds and fevers began to spread among the soldiers. When it started to rain towards the end of the year the trenches collected water and the earth at the bottom turned to mud. So instead of digging into the earth to seek protection, the soldiers had to build defences that stood on the soggy ground. The Germans used barrels that they had found in the brewery. They filled the barrels with earth and built a wall. It gave protection, at least against rifle bullets.

"So the end of the first year of the war came nearer and with it Christmas," wrote Johannes Niemann. "The Emperor had promised us that we would be home with our mothers for Christmas, but unfortunately this did not happen."

⊜ JIMMY ⊜

Back into the trenches

When the 93rd came out of Ploegsteert Wood on 13 November after the attack over the field, there remained 48 days of 1914. The battalion spent 32 of these days in the trenches, first 25 days, then seven days, and during this time it lost 20 soldiers, 19 wounded and one killed. Forty-two of these days were free of casualties. After all that had happened during the war this period seems to have been quiet, but this was not the case. What went on was an activity where, during one and a half months, there were six days when one or more of the participants were injured, perhaps for life. And one of them was killed. It would be wrong to write that this was a calm time even if other times during the autumn had been more terrible.

The battalion was in trenches near the town of Houplines in France, near the border with Belgium. The companies took turns to be at the front. Those who were not there were at work elsewhere, usually digging.

During this time the soldiers learnt to work and to live in the trenches. The ditches across the fields had now been dug so deep that the soldiers could stand upright without showing their heads to German snipers. But there were not yet ditches for walking to the front. Soldiers on their way to or from the front trenches must either crawl and hide behind undulations in the ground or take a chance and run over open spaces.

The trenches were dug in a zigzag pattern in order to limit the damage from exploding shells and to make it impossible to shoot from the side with a machine gun along the entire line of defence. Soldiers dug holes into the walls of the trenches, where they were a little more, but not fully, protected from grenades. In their holes they could lie down for a rest and get away from the mud. They used doors and timber from destroyed houses behind the front to build roofs and floors. Sometimes they would also bring some straw on which to lie.

Besides the task to defend themselves the soldiers' most important job was to strengthen their trenches and to get rid of the water. Much of the time was spent repairing damage to the trenches. German artillery shells often exploded in the trenches or nearby causing the walls and dugouts to collapse, but it was the rain that caused most of the damage. Aidan Liddell, an officer who at this time had become commander of the machine guns, noticed on 9 December that the rain had ruined the front of the trench so that it no longer gave them protection against bullets and that the Germans knew this.

All through the winter the soldiers splashed in water and mud in the trenches. Kilted soldiers had a special reason to notice the depth of water. When the water level rose it happened that their kilts floated around their legs.

The soldiers must have had wet feet most of the time and many suffered from trench foot. This was the name of the condition caused by walking in water and mud for a long time without being able to dry one's feet. Trench foot could deteriorate into gangrene so that soldiers' toes or feet had to be amputated. The Second Battalion of the Royal Welch Fusiliers, which was in the same brigade as the 93rd, fought these injuries successfully with the help of the battalion's cooks. They collected leftover grease from the cooking and sent it up to the trenches. After stand-to each morning, when all soldiers stood ready with their rifles, the soldiers smeared each other's feet with the grease.

At the end of November there was frost for a few days. The mud at the bottom of the trenches froze, which was a relief, but the soldiers also suffered in the cold weather. Most of them were barelegged under their kilts. Some made leggings from sandbags, but many soldiers were frostbitten.

They could only make small fires with coke or small splinters

The soldiers fought ceaselessly against water. The picture shows a British pump at la Boutillerie, near Lille, in December 1914. The 93rd held trenches here after the fight at Le Maisnil.
(Imperial War Museum, Q049221)

from food boxes. Bigger fires were not allowed. Their smoke was visible during the day and their light was visible at night. So it was difficult to cook.

In the middle of December, James Jack became commander of a company in the First Battalion of the Scottish Rifles, another battalion in the 93rd's brigade. When he came to his company he wrote that it was impossible to dig shelters into the walls of the trenches. The soldiers had no roof except their waterproof sheets, which they put up for protection. Parcels from home offered some relief from the harsh conditions. Friends and relatives sent food, sweets, tobacco and knitted socks, caps, scarves and sweaters.

Some soldiers were lucky to find something that eased the suffering. Frank Collier and three other soldiers were sent out on guard duty in a deserted café. When they searched the house they found coal and a spring mattress. "We got an extra ration each of rum, making plenty of toddy and making merry all night."

But this was an exception. Conditions in the trenches were punishing. Most of us would not cope out there in a muddy ditch with wet boots, wet clothes, with some straw on a door for a bed and with a slimy hole in the ground for a toilet. The soldiers were lousy in the original meaning of the word. They could not wash or shave. They smelled and the trench smelled. Most of them had badly worn clothes and they were often caked with half dried mud, both on their clothes and on their bare legs. Among illnesses recorded in the 93rd are pneumonia, rheumatism, sunstroke, piles, gonorrhoea, frostbite, defective teeth and nervous debility.

To add to this was the risk of tetanus. James Jack wrote in December that "tetanus is a great danger in this highly cultivated land. All casualties, however slight, are now immediately inoculated against it."

And all the time there was the risk of being wounded or killed by a sniper, by a grenade or in an attack. Aidan Liddell described trench warfare in a letter in December:

"We hear most gruesome stories (a little tall I think)... All the ground is full of dead bodies, and when the wall of a dug-out or part of the trench falls in, there is generally a body exposed."

But when the soldiers in the 93rd dug a new trench a few weeks later they found that the stories about dead soldiers coming out of the ground unfortunately were not so tall.

The Scots realized that the Germans opposite also suffered. Three German soldiers came over and gave themselves up. They said that they had only one meal each day. But they said also that the Germans had more guns and more soldiers in their trenches than the British.

Aidan Liddell described how both sides attacked and perhaps managed to take one of the enemy's trenches. But then there was a counterattack and those who had made the first attack were forced to withdraw and go back to their old trench.

"However the result is a heavy casualty list, and the positions as they were in the beginning. Seems pretty hopeless, doesn't it?"

Aidan Liddell had applied for leave to go home to England. He was seventh in line among the officers although he had not joined the battalion until 7 September. Not many of the officers who came with the battalion to Boulogne in August remained; those who should have been in front of Aidan Liddell in the line.

King George V came to visit the British troops in the first days of December. Jimmy Coyle was chosen to represent the battalion at a parade. The others in the group were one officer, five other non-commissioned officers and two privates. They marched to a village a few miles behind the front. A group from the Second Battalion in the Royal Welch Fusiliers, in the same brigade as the 93rd, was also in the parade. One of its soldiers wrote: "The parade was spick and span without, but most verminous underneath."

The war diary of the 93rd says that a sergeant in the group was at the parade to receive a medal from the king for his conduct at Le Maisnil. No reasons are given for the other members of the group to explain why they were picked to represent the battalion, so we don't know why Jimmy Coyle was there. It could have been a reward because he was a good soldier and a way for the commander to express his appreciation. But it could also have been because his clothes were less worn than the clothes of the soldiers who spent their days in the trenches. Or maybe the commander dared not send away too many soldiers whose jobs were to man the guns.

Towards the end of December the Christmas mail started to flood the battalion with parcels and letters. Aidan Liddell noticed that there was less military activity. There were two reasons; the Christmas atmosphere and the rain.

The 93rd was ordered to march to the trenches on the evening of 20 December. Aidan Liddell walked out during the day to look at the machine gun emplacements in daylight. The trenches were wetter than ever before. Henry Hyslop wrote that "mud is well over the top of one's boots."

The war diary of the 93rd does not note where these trenches were, other than near Houplines. But their position is clearly written in the war diary of the first battalion of the Middlesex regiment. This was the battalion that the 93rd relieved. The Middlesex battalion had been in these trenches – "in a fearful state of mud" – since 25 November. When they came there they recorded their position in their war diary: "E and N.E. of Houplines and about 800x [yards] away." Aidan Liddell wrote later that the distance to the Germans varied between 80 and 500 yards.

With the help of a map in Johannes Niemann's book it is possible to say, with reasonable certainty, precisely where this position was. The map shows the situation after the fighting in October. After that the trenches were not much altered for a long time. Johannes Niemann has written by hand a name on the map northeast of Houplines, right behind the British line in the area where the 93rd took over on 20 December. I asked Dominiek Dendooven, a historian at the museum In Flanders Fields in Ypres, to help me read Johannes Niemann's handwriting. The name is: "Ferme la Moutarderie" (The Mustard Factory Farm). This farm is no longer there but with the help of the shape of the old road it is possible to point out where it was. The road is marked on Johannes Niemann's map and it is also on a modern map, even if the traffic now runs on new roads. In the maps of 1914 this farm has no name, but a house a few hundred metres to the north has the name "La Moutarderie" (The Mustard Factory). It is reasonable to think that the Saxons used this name when they named the farm.

"Ferme la Moutarderie" is the only name that Johannes

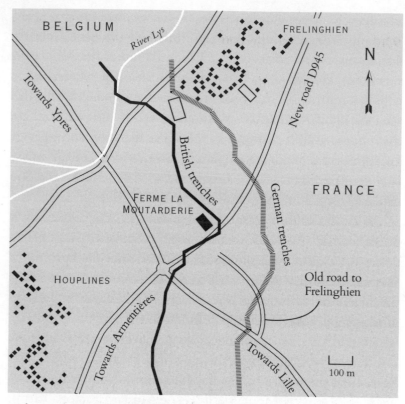

The 93rd spent Christmas in trenches near Houplines. Near the village and right behind the British trench was a ruined farm. The Germans had named it Ferme la Moutarderie (The Mustard Factory Farm). This is probably the farm where some of the 93rd's officers lived in the cellar. See also aerial photo on pages 172-173.

Niemann has written by the lines of trenches in the map, but he did not write why this farm was interesting. It might have been that it stuck out like a nose from the British line, like a landmark. But the reason for Johannes Niemann's interest might also have been that this was the farm where some officers of the 93rd moved in when the Battalion took over the trenches on 20 December.

Henry Hyslop wrote in his diary for that day: "As second in command I have now to be in the trenches, or at least at the end of a telephone, so I have taken up my abode in the cellar of a farm just behind B Company's trenches. The farm has nearly all been..." – and there the entry ends because the next page in the

Henry Hyslop kept a detailed diary during the war. Some of the officers lived in this cellar at Christmas, under a ruined farm right behind the trenches. It is probably Ferme la Moutarderie that Johannes Niemann had marked on his map. Frederick Chandler, the Battalion doctor, took this picture on Christmas Day.
(Frederick Chandler, Imperial War Museum, HU128734)

diary is missing. But the sentence probably ended something like this: "...destroyed by shells." Aidan Liddell also wrote about the farm in a letter: "We have a farmhouse just behind the trench, where the officers of the company nearest take meals, an excellent cellar vaulted over..." He shared a cow byre with another officer, where they slept in "plenty of straw and no mud."

There is also a photograph of Henry Hyslop sitting at a table in this cellar on Christmas Day. A copy of the picture is in his diary and it is also in doctor Frederick Chandler's photo album. The doctor took the picture. It was also in this cellar that the officers at the front had their Christmas dinner, so Jimmy Coyle must have been there on duty.

I believe that the Germans knew that this cellar was a British command post and that this was the reason it was practical to give it a name, the name that Johannes Niemann wrote in the map in his book.

What is certain is that it was in these fields that the Saxons in IR133 and the Scots in the 93rd spent Christmas.

Christmas Truce

A quiet Christmas

Thousands of soldiers climbed out of their trenches during the Christmas Truce. They met in No Man's Land, shook hands, offered each other something good to drink and something good to smoke. They exchanged souvenirs.

That was not strange at all. There was nothing strange with thousands of young men, who did dangerous jobs in terrible conditions, meeting for the holiday. It was quite natural that they met and wished each other Merry Christmas. What is strange is that they had tried to shoot each other to death a few days earlier. And what is even more strange is that some time later they would carry on shooting and then try to kill maybe the very men they had recently shaken hands with.

The Christmas Truce was just natural. No one ordered the soldiers to stop shooting. No one organized the great truce, neither the generals nor some common grass roots movement among the soldiers. But some high commanders might have contributed to enlarge the truce. Both before Christmas and when the truce was going on they sent out orders sharply forbidding fraternization. They also threatened with punishment those who sought contact with the enemy or accepted a truce offered by the enemy. Like other bans, these orders might have made fraternization more tempting. If it was worth banning it probably was something one would like to do.

What also shows that the truce was quite natural was that it was not one big truce. It was many truces, maybe a hundred truces.

When a soldier on the Western Front looked at the horizon he usually did not see beyond a pile of earth at the edge of the trench or maybe some sandbags. It must have been very difficult to observe what happened opposite one's own trench, maybe with the help of a tiny periscope. Anyone who put his head up risked being killed by a sniper. Therefore it happened that soldiers in one trench did not notice that soldiers nearby had a truce and were out in No Man's Land. And when there was a truce soldiers might have been surprised when they looked out of their ditch to find people walking between trenches both on the left and to the right.

The battalion holding trenches south of the 93rd at Christmas was the first battalion of the Scottish Rifles, which also belonged to the 19th Brigade. James Jack was one of the company commanders in this battalion. He heard the Prussians opposite sing and he heard Scots and Prussians call out to each other, mostly insults. One German, who must have noticed the Scots' caps called out: "When will you return to Maryhill Barracks?" This was the barracks in Glasgow where Jimmy Coyle had lived before the war and where the battalion team had played football. But James Jack had no thought of a truce and did not notice that the neighbours had one. The fighting went on. In his diary entry for Boxing Day he wrote: "Sergeant Buss and Lance Corporal

The soldiers used periscopes to look out into No Man's Land without having to expose their heads to enemy snipers. The field of vision was narrow. That is why one battalion might not notice that the next battalion was celebrating Christmas together with their opponents out in the field. (Argyll and Sutherland Highlanders)

Gibb of A Company set out last night, of their own free will, to try to capture a German machine gun. Neither has returned (Gibb was killed)."

Not until 13 January did he write about the Christmas Truce: "There are extraordinary stories of unofficial Christmas truces with the enemy."

So when the war fell silent on Christmas Eve or Christmas Day it was because many soldiers took this initiative without

Thousands of German and British soldiers climbed out of their trenches on Christmas Day to meet the enemy soldiers and wish them Happy Christmas.
(Bridgeman Art Library)

knowing that others at the same time took the same initiative. Each of them decided that the natural thing was to stop shooting.

In their book *Christmas Truce,* Malcolm Brown and Shirley Seaton write that the Christmas Truce could "make even dedicated professional soldiers see, if only briefly, the whole idea of war in a new light – or at any rate glimpse the thought that war might not be as natural to an intelligent species as had always been assumed."

This is how the professional soldier James Jack thought. When he heard about the Christmas Truce he wrote:

"These incidents seem to suggest that, except in the temper of battle or some great grievance, educated men have no desire to kill one another; and that were it not for aggressive National Policies, or the fear of them by others, war between civilized peoples would seldom take place."

Many soldiers wrote home after Christmas to tell about the truce. Several wrote that it was difficult to believe what had happened. One soldier wrote: "Just you think that while you were eating your turkey, etc., I was out talking and shaking hands with the very men I hade been trying to kill a few hours before!! It was astounding!"

It was difficult to describe the truce with words. So E.R.P. Berryman, a British officer in the Indian regiment Garhwal Rifles, made a drawing instead. It is in a letter dated 1 January 1915. No one has better described the difference between the days of war and the truce.

E.R.P. Berryman also used words in his letter. He wrote: "It was most amusing and so utterly out of keeping with the rest of the show we can hardly realize it happened."

This is the drawing that the officer E.R.P. Berryman sent to
his family to describe the Christmas Truce.
(Imperial War Museum)

His army corps had a rest period behind the front and he
expected to get leave to go home.

"Isn't it ripping and all being well I'll be home today week,
on the 8th, sometime during the evening so anything I don't

tell you in this letter I can tell you then ...[I'll] leave again on the morning of the 14th. Just five full days at home."

E.R.P Berryman's unit had been "in those bally old trenches" for 25 days and during that time he had not shaved. But now he had had a bath in a dustbin and he felt clean and smart in a new uniform. Still this was his first wish for a welcome at home:

"I hope you'll have a nice hot bath waiting for me."

Around Christmas, the British held some 20 miles of the front almost at its northern end at the border between France and Belgium. (France held almost 400 miles of front.) Malcolm Brown and Shirley Seaton who have made the most thorough study of the truce, estimate that fighting ceased on two thirds of the British front. French and Belgian units also had truces with the Germans, but they were not at all as common as among the British.

Many of the German units that took initiatives for truces came from Saxony. The Saxons had a better reputation among the British than the Prussians and British newspapers made a difference between Saxons and Prussians. "Prussians", however, were not always Prussians. Battalions and regiments known to be aggressive were called "Prussians" wherever they came from.

The British felt close to the Saxons because their own forefathers were Saxons. The story of King Alfred the Great, who was the first king to call himself Anglo-Saxon and who defended England against the Vikings, is a part of the country's nation-building story. The British soldiers also might have felt they had their own "family" in the trenches opposite because Queen Victoria's husband Albert had been of Saxon descent.

Furthermore, the Saxons were not blamed for the stories of atrocities against the civilian population in Belgium at the beginning of the war. But that was wrong. It was soldiers from the Saxon Third Army, where Albert Schmidt's Regiment IR133 belonged, who attacked the Belgian town of Dinant on 23 August and then killed more than 600 civilians. But this did not ruin the Christmas Truce. The Saxons came out even better during the chats in No Man's Land when they said they also disliked the Prussians.

In most places the truce began in the evening of Christmas Eve and it was mostly the Germans who took the initiative. Many truces were spontaneous, while others were planned. The officer Kurt Zehmisch in the 134th Infantry Regiment, whose diary is one of the best on the German side, wrote that his unit went out to the trenches on Christmas Eve.

"I have given orders to my people that today in the holy night and on Christmas Day no shot will be fired from our side if it can be avoided ...No sooner did we man the trenches than we (we and the English) tried to make contact. First we whistled and they answered."

Kurt Zehmisch was a teacher of languages and could speak English, and so could one of the soldiers. They called out to the English soldiers, who were in trenches just over 100 yards away. Soon a conversation was going on. It seems it was full of banter, but still friendly. The Germans wanted to meet the English half way between the trenches to exchange cigarettes. Two German soldiers went out through the wire entanglements, which stood ten yards in front of the trenches. Two Englishmen came from the other side. They walked slowly in a ditch full of willows.

Both sides had assured that the soldiers would not carry weapons and that no one would shoot.

"Soldiers in the trenches on both sides followed tensely what was going to happen," Kurt Zehmisch wrote.

Finally the Englishmen came out of the ditch. They held their hands high and one of them had a cap full of English cigarettes and tobacco. The Englishmen came up to the Germans, wished them a merry Christmas and the soldiers shook hands.

"At that the English in their trenches and we clapped our hands and shouted enthusiastically 'Bravo'!"

After that they exchanged cigarettes for cigars, they lit one each and stood there talking for a long time. One of the English turned to the German trenches and called out: "I wish you a Merry Christmas and a Happy New Year!" Kurt Zehmisch and the others called back: "Thank you very much, I wish you the same!" Then the same greeting came with a roar from the English at the other side of the field.

The meeting ended with an agreement not to shoot during the night nor the next day, Christmas Day. The four soldiers out there in the darkness shook hands again and said goodbye. When the Germans came back their comrades had many questions to ask and then they shared the English cigarettes. On the edges of their trenches were candles and Christmas trees. "It was like a festival of light," Kurt Zehmisch wrote. They sang and played and the Englishmen showed their appreciation with shouts and applause.

"Not a shot was fired on our part of the front, but to the left of us the 106th [Infantry regiment] kept up a stupid shooting all night long."

"Like most of my men I was awake the whole night. It was a wonderful night, though a bit cold."

Along other trenches truces started in the same way. The Germans put up candles and Christmas trees. A British soldier thought they looked like footlights in a theatre. The enemies bandied words across No Man's Land, soldiers climbed out of their trenches and met. Before they went back to their own lines they agreed: "We won't shoot if you don't shoot." Then the night went on with songs from both sides, some sung together, like duets.

On the morning of Christmas Day it was still mostly quiet. It was cold and a large part of the British front was covered by fog that lifted at midday. It was a day with Christmas card weather. The soldiers came out of their trenches. They enjoyed being able to walk and to look around. They did not need to splash through mud, because it was now frozen.

Several of Kurt Zemisch's soldiers went out to greet the English. He went out himself and met a couple of British officers. Meanwhile the soldiers dug graves for Germans and Englishmen who had been lying dead for a long time. But this does not seem to have put a dampener on things. One German non-commissioned officer got groups of soldiers from both sides together and took pictures with his camera.

"All this was so wonderful and strange. So thought also the English officers."

In many places there was a throng of soldiers out there between the trenches. But everybody was not out to talk to the enemy. Some soldiers took the opportunity to collect firewood or take potatoes from the fields. I have not seen an estimate for how many took part but thousands is no exaggeration. They

The photographs from the Christmas Truce are classics in the histories of both war and photography. The name of the British soldier (third from the left) was Andrew. The soldier looking over the shoulder was J. Selby Grigg. They belonged to the London Rifle Brigade. The Germans came from the Saxon army corps where also Albert Schmidt's IR133 belonged. (Imperial War Museum, Q011745)

talked, sometimes in English, more seldom in German, often with signs or with the assistance of those who could speak a bit of the opponents' language. Enemies shook hands, exchanged souvenirs, food or drinks. They showed their family photographs. It is remarkable how many had cameras. They took group pictures with German and British soldiers, sometimes wearing each other's caps. In one place British officers said they would arrange a new truce at New Year so the Germans could see if the pictures came out well. The mail service was sometimes excellent and it was quite possible to send a film roll home for development and get the pictures back in a week. Some of the pictures survive. They are classics both in the history of war and the history of photography.

Several funny and moving stories are told about meetings in No Man's Land. One soldier from London recognized his barber among the Germans. The barber got out his scissors, placed his customer on an ammunition box and gave him a trimming. Then he finished his job with a razor. "And maybe I should cut your throat today, yes? Save ammunition tomorrow." British barbers were also busy, cropping heads of German soldiers who kneeled on the frozen mud. A German juggler, who had performed in London, drew a large crowd.

Both the barbers and the juggler found their ways into the literature of the Christmas Truce. One of the barbers was a member of the British officer Bruce Bairnsfather's machine gun team. Bairnsfather was a cartoonist and his charachter Old Bill became a representative for all Tommies on the Western Front. Bruce Bairnsfather, who survived the war, wrote that he remembered a patient German kneeling to have his hair cut by the machine gun barber. In one of his cartoons Old Bill gives another soldier a haircut, but he is a British comrade and the job is done in their trench. The juggler appears in Robert Graves' short story *Christmas Truce*. Robert Graves came into the war after the Christmas Truce, but he heard stories about it. He also survived the war and published his story in 1962.

Many of the stories about the Christmas Truce are about food and drink. The Second Battalion of the Royal Welch Fusiliers, who were next to Jimmy Coyle's battalion, to the north, received two barrels of beer from the Germans. The barrels came from the brewery in Frelinghien. The Welch accepted the beer, but found it thin. In other battalions soldiers were given sauerkraut for chocolate, shared a big pot of meat made from British tins and cooked a pig in No Man's Land. One British soldier managed to trade a lot of tinned meat and jam for a pickelhaube, a German helmet. The day after, the German called for his counterpart. He needed to borrow the helmet for an inspection. But then he returned it, so the story goes.

But the sorrows of war made themselves known. Hugo Klemm, in Albert Schmidt's regiment, wrote that an English soldier gave him a cap badge. It was probably a Scot, because he was opposite Jimmy Coyle's battalion. The cap badge had belonged to one of the Scot's friends who had been killed.

The Christmas Truce opened up chances to ask the enemies if they knew what had happened to missing soldiers and to return medals and personal belongings from those who had died at a dressing station or in a hospital on the enemy side. Esslemont Adams, a chaplain with the Gordon Highlanders, went out in No Man's Land and found a German officer. When they had talked for a while the German took out his notebook. He had written the name of a British officer who had been mortally wounded on the German side. The German had seen that the British officer tried to take something out of his pocket. The German helped him, saw that it was a photograph of the dying officer's wife and held it in front of him until he died a few minutes later. The chaplain wrote down the name and address so that he could write a letter to the widow.

Esslemont Adams also took the initiative to conduct a funeral that is the best known of all that took place, thanks to several accounts. In this place there were just some 50 yards between the trenches, where dead German and British soldiers lay. They were now carried to their side of the halfway line and their comrades started digging their graves. The British soldiers made crosses from wooden biscuit boxes. A Scottish officer found 29 of the soldiers whom he had led in an attack on 18 December. He searched their pockets and took care of their personal belongings and took their identity discs. It was "heart rendering" he wrote in the battalion war diary. He also ordered the dead soldiers' rifles to be collected, but the Germans did not allow that. Rifles on their side of the halfway line were spoils of war.

The soldiers dug altogether around 100 graves among the cabbages in the field. The Germans formed up on their side and the British on their side. Everyone took off their caps. Esslemont Adams read the texts in English and a German divinity student read them in German. After the ceremony there was silence for a while. Esslemont Adams went up to the German commander, saluted, shook his hand and bade farewell.

High commanders on each side banned trucing and fraternization. These orders came both in good time before Christmas and when the Christmas Truce was underway. The generals feared that truces or silent agreements not to shoot would affect the soldiers' fighting spirit. Both sides also warned their commanders in the trenches that the enemy would make use of the festivities and launch attacks. A British general, who had a report about the truces was angry and burst out: "Christ Almighty!" In the next moment he realized what he had said.

There were also officers, at least on the British side, who were against the whole celebration of Christmas. One reason was that Christmas letters and gifts blocked the transport routes so that war materiel could not reach the front. There were hundreds of thousands of parcels and hundreds of thousands of letters from the soldiers' friends and families. Lady Rawlinson, married to the British general Henry Rawlinson, sent a plum pudding to each of the soldiers in her husband's corps. Many of these probably ended up in German hands and mouths after the trading during Christmas. There came also hundreds of thousands of Christmas cards and presents from the Royal family. All soldiers received a metal box with tobacco or candy. They came from a fund, named after the king's daughter Mary and her picture was on the lid.

The soldiers clearly knew or suspected that commanders would clamp down on truces. In some places, therefore, the soldiers posted watch-outs behind the front to warn against staff officers. The author Maxtone Graham wrote in 1965 about such an alarm when a brigadier was coming to the front trenches. At a given signal soldiers disappeared from No Man's Land, sentries in the trenches gazed through their holes, the machine guns were manned. When the brigadier came there was no sign that the war was not fought as usual, except perhaps a lingering scent of German cigars. Henry Rawlinson told that a German colleague had been fooled in much the same way. A German called over to the British: "Look out – we have a General coming down to the trenches so we must fire for an hour." At these occasions the fire from each side was usually carefully aimed at the treetops behind the enemy.

Henry Rawlinson was one of the high commanders who did not clamp down on the Christmas Truce. He realized that the pause in the fighting made it possible to improve the defences and in particular he mentioned work to clear out ditches so that water could run from the trenches. Other officers took the opportunity to see the enemy line. A British artillery officer put on a German uniform and looked around the German trenches. He saw where the Germans had positioned their machine guns. One soldier told that he had smoked a cigar with the best sniper in the German Army, who had killed many Britons. He had found out where the sniper had his hole and intended to "down" him the next day.

One of the few British officers who was disciplined for taking part in the truce tried to plead with his superiors, telling them how much information he had gained thanks to being able to walk around in No Man's Land. He pleaded in vain. He lost his place in the line for leave and he was killed before he had a new chance to come home.

The Germans also tried to gain information. A British sergeant drew a large crowd when he appeared in No Man's Land dressed in a skirt that he had found in an abandoned house. While this drag show caught the attention, two British officers saw a German edging nearer to the British trenches. They walked beside him and shooed him away until he got fed up and returned to his own side.

But there were instances when both German and British soldiers came to the opponent's trenches, sometimes because they were invited, sometimes because they were drunk. Several soldiers were taken prisoner to prevent them from reporting back about things such as where the machine guns were positioned. This is the way the truce ended in one place on New Year's Day, 1 January. Four British soldiers were detained by the Germans. The British retaliated and made 40 visiting Germans prisoners of war. Then the war started again.

Many of the truce agreements were in force during Christmas Day. But it was far from easy to get the war started again. One German soldier has told that an officer on Christmas Day threatened to shoot one of his own soldiers who refused to shoot at the British. Soldiers on both sides had silent agreements and therefore it was quiet at the front. Henry Rawlinson wrote about the truce as late as 10 January without being annoyed. In one place the truce lasted until Easter, which was in April. But in January it was not Christmas but the rain and mud that made it difficult or impossible to continue the war. Horace Smith-Dorrien, one of the generals who had been most angry when he got reports about the Christmas Truce, wrote in his diary in the middle of January:

"Two unfortunate Cameron Highlanders disappeared in a morass, one was never found and the other died on being recovered. I am afraid that a young officer of the RFA has also been lost in the same way."

The war went on.

ALBERT AND JIMMY

Delicious silence

Also along that part of the front where IR133 and the 93rd held trenches opposite each other it was the Saxons who started the Christmas Truce. There are several accounts about Saxon soldiers being aware that they had Anglo-Saxons opposite. Johannes Niemann had the same thought and wrote about it in his book:

"What was happening? And where did it happen? Not everywhere, but mainly on the front in Flanders where Saxon regiments were, perhaps also because Tommies looked upon us Saxons as the forefathers of the Anglo-Saxons."

British soldiers were called Tommies, both by themselves and by the Germans. The German soldiers were called Fritz. Johannes Niemann seems not to have made any difference between Englishmen and Scots, who were sometimes called Jocks. He probably did not realize that many of the soldiers in the 93rd were not Anglo-Saxons but had their forefathers among the Celts.

Here I would like to stop to explain how we can be sure that these two units, the 93rd and IR133, met at Christmas and why Jimmy Coyle and Albert Schmidt most probably were there. As for the Scots there is no problem. The war diary and two other accounts say that the Scots met soldiers from the 133rd regiment. Johannes Niemann said and wrote that the British soldiers opposite wore kilts. So they must have been soldiers in the 93rd because the British soldiers in the neighbouring battalions on both sides wore trousers. As for the Saxons, Johannes Niemann wrote that

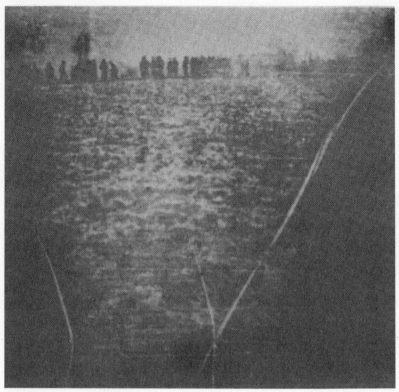

One of the Germans used binoculars to take this picture of the truce
between IR133 and the 93rd on Christmas Day.
(From Johannes Niemann's book)

they were in this area between Armentières and Frelinghien and
he wrote that they had Scots opposite. The book *Christmas Truce*
says that IR133 was divided and that some soldiers were further
to the north. This was probably the second battalion, which had
earlier been lent to another regiment. Johannes Niemann was
in the third battalion, so he was at Frelinghien and there is no

information about the first battalion, with Albert Schmidt, being anywhere else.

IR133 were in billets behind the front on 24 December when they were ordered to leave and to spend Christmas in the trenches. The day before they had celebrated Christmas together with local people, Johannes Niemann told. The night was still and starry. In the book *Christmas Truce* he said:

"We marched forward to the trenches like Father Christmas with parcels hanging from us. All was quiet. No shooting."

Hugo Klemm, an intelligence officer in the regimental staff, says in *Christmas Truce* that their commander gave a stern warning before they went out to the trenches on Christmas evening: "He emphasized that for that day and following days special alertness would be required, as it was expected that the English would perhaps take advantage of our good mood at Christmas by mounting a raid." But the soldiers had no intention to allow vigilance to get in the way of the celebration of Christmas.

"Several of my chums had been able to get hold of two small Christmas trees complete with candles, to be mounted on the parapet of the trenches, while others dragged planks, fascines (bundles of brushwood), etc. with them, to be used in the battle against water and mud. As was usual at that time, having settled in the trenches, we fired the occasional shot from our outposts to let the enemy know we would not let ourselves be surprised."

But this was just a formality. When it was finished, the Germans mounted their Christmas trees on the edge of the trench and lit the candles. Hugo Klemm wrote that there were lighted Christmas trees on the German line as far as he could see.

Hugo Klemm also reported that one German non-commissioned officer walked out with a Christmas tree into No Man's Land. A British soldier came out to meet him, in spite of warnings shouted to him by his comrades. But the Saxon and British soldiers met and shook hands. When the British soldier had got back to his trench, his comrades applauded the magnanimity of the Germans, Hugo Klemm said.

Johannes Niemann, who was platoon commander, sat together with his company commander and their orderlies in their dugout, which was a cave in the earth next to the trench. They sang their German Christmas songs. Suddenly a fusillade broke out. They soon understood why. The Scots opposite thought that the Christmas trees with the burning candles were part of some trickery, so they shot for safety's sake. But soon they saw that it was just Christmas trees and stopped shooting. After that nobody fired a shot all through the night. Instead Christmas songs started to drift over No Man's Land. Instead of the usual shooting contest they had a singing contest.

At Christmas 1968, Johannes Niemann told what happened in the BBC film *Christmas Day Passed Quietly*: "We sang our old Christmas songs, 'Stille Nacht, heilige Nacht'. [Tommies sang] 'A long way to Tipperary', 'Home, sweet home'." The spirit of Christmas on both sides was more powerful than the spirit of war.

Next day the war seems to have been forgotten, he wrote in his book. At midday his orderly burst into his dugout and reported that friends and foes were out between the trenches.

"One glance over there and there were the Christmas presents being handed out. Had peace broken out? What should I do? I thought quickly about it and then I ran out myself. Soon I was in the middle of the throng."

Everybody shook hands and swapped what they had – tobacco, chocolate, schnapps, badges and medal ribbons. Scots and Saxons together chased hares that for a long time had lived in No Man's Land undisturbed by humans.

In the BBC film Johannes Niemann gave more details. He was out in the field where Scottish and Saxon soldiers "began to shake hands and clap each other on the shoulder".

"We spoke about the things the soldier has on his mind, about families and naturally about the mademoiselles in Armantières and Lille."

From the other side Doctor Frederick Chandler described in a letter how the truce began on Christmas Eve. The front fell silent. "It was a most delicious feeling." He apologized in his letter for using this word so many times, "but I know no other word to describe it".

Doctor Chandler also described the weather: "It was a bright starry moonlit night and it froze hard." It was quiet. Soon Saxons and Scots were heard shouting to each other. Then there was music from the German trenches and they sang. A corporal among the Scots, the Doctor wrote in his diary, shouted across that he wanted one of the Saxons to come out halfway for a fight. The answer came, with a Glasgow accent: "No, but I'll come oot and meet ye." This Saxon soldier had worked in Scotland. They both went out in No Man's Land, exchanged souvenirs and talked about Christmas.

There is also another story about how the truce started between the 93rd and IR133. It was told by the officer Ian

Stewart in the book *Christmas Truce*. Ian Stewart was 19 years old and he is most likely the officer that Frederick Chandler later in a magazine article described as "little S, our baby subaltern."

Ian Stewart wrote that the Saxons put candles on the edges of their trenches. They urged the Scots to come out and the opponents agreed to send out two men each. Ian Stewart volunteered.

"I could talk some German and one of the German officers some English. He was about my age. Our conversation was no different from that of meeting a friendly opponent at a football match. He ...gave me a cigar to which I was unaccustomed and which nearly made me sick... My gift was a tin of bully beef from my emergency ration, the best thing available. After 10 minutes we said a friendly goodbye and returned to our lines and relative normality."

It is impossible to say which of these stories is true. They both come from reliable sources. Probably both are true. Although there was moonlight it must have been difficult for one company to see what happened in front of another company.

On the morning of Christmas Day it was foggy and still cold. Doctor Chandler walked towards the front from the battalion headquarters, which were a few hundred yards behind. He wanted to take a few pictures of the front trenches. Much of the mud was still frozen, the Doctor wrote, "but the communication trenches were practically impassable." So he walked on a road confident that the German snipers could not see him in the fog. Still "several bullets came unpleasantly near, and I began to regret not having braved the slush of the communication trench, but as our commanding officer used to say, expressing the views of the men on the matter 'If you go up the communication trench you are bound to get your feet wet, whereas the worst that can happen to you if you go along on the top is to get shot'."

Doctor Chandler sought cover from the bullets and waited until no more bullets came near. When he continued his walk towards the front he saw the boots of a German soldier sticking out of the earth by the side of the road. He called some soldiers who were near.

"I called attention to the legs, and investigation showed the rest of the gentleman imperfectly covered with earth; so he was popped into a more comfortable grave – a proceeding which delights the heart of every true British soldier."

Frederick Chandler, the 93rd's battalion doctor, walked to the front on Christmas Day to take photographs of the soldiers in the trenches. They were "narrow, uncomfortable places," he wrote.
(Frederick Chandler, Imperial War Museum, HU128733)

But first they took some buttons from the uniform as souvenirs.

"'Rest in peace, poor Fritz', thought I; it is not you or your like that have caused all this; there is not a private soldier in any of the combatant armies who would not make peace tomorrow."

The doctor reached the front trenches. They were narrow and uncomfortable. Many soldiers "were tortured by rheumatic pains and frozen feet and infected by lice." Every evening many who were sick came to the doctor. He sent everybody back to the trenches, except the worst cases.

"This was one of the most trying and painful parts of one's work. It was not, 'Is this man ill?' but, 'Which is the most ill?'"

The doctor also described the tension that the men had to live with: "Never was there a moment's respite; at any moment of the night or day the causal shelling or sniping might develop into that awful roar, or the darkness beyond be filled with the silent approach of a thousand bayonets."

Scots have told that the German snipers were active in the morning of Christmas Day, like any other day. But at midday "the most amazing thing occurred," Doctor Chandler wrote. The firing stopped. Once again the soldiers shouted back and forth and then some Saxons looked up over the edge of their trench.

Frank Collier, in A Company, wrote about Christmas Day in the regimental magazine in 1965. At midday he heard soldiers call out: "The Jerries are out of their trench!" Jerry was another of the British soldiers' names for the Germans.

"I can tell you – we were on the fire step like lightning – our rifles in our hands, bayonets fixed and our fingers pretty near the trigger. Then we saw they were really unarmed and shouting and waving their arms; we could hardly believe our eyes. The order came along, 'Stand To, but hold your fire.' As they came slowly forward it would be hard to describe our feelings. They would be about halfway towards our trenches when someone shouted: 'Look! Some of our men are out in the open too.' Our fellows were unarmed out there, and quite a number of us joined them."

A few soldiers remained in the trench, ready with their rifles. The rest went out in No Man's Land. Soon there was a mixed crowd of soldiers in the middle of the field. They talked, shook hands and started to exchange gifts. A knitted cap, possibly just arrived in a parcel from home, would go for a grey German field cap. A tobacco ration or a few British tins of meat perhaps went for cigars.

Scots and Saxons talked although many of them did not understand what the soldiers on the other side said. But a few Saxons spoke English quite well. Henry Hyslop noted that they "looked very cheery but were mostly quite young and had few officers." They talked about the war, how it would end. The Saxons were convinced that the Russians were beaten and that the Germans would successfully end the war on the Western Front in the summer, at the latest. Henry Hyslop asked if they really hated the English as much as was said, "but they said it was quite untrue and they were not Prussians."

Frank Collier thought the Germans looked "crumby". Some had uniforms that did not fit. He suspected they were officers posing as soldiers so that they could get closer to the British trenches and spy. "But we kept them halfway at every point."

According to the war diary of the 93rd, Scots also wanted to see the opponents' trenches: "The position was reconnoitred by Lieut Anderson." This entry can only mean that Lieutenant Anderson managed to get close to the German line and could see things that the Scots did not know about.

Trading was difficult for Frank Collier because he was not a smoker and he had no tobacco to offer. Instead he offered a piece of soap. "He gave me a quizzical look, as much as to say: 'Do you think I'm crumby?' Ah, well, all of them looked crumby – so did we."

"One wit in our group noticed their belt buckles with the motto 'Gott Mit Uns', pointing to a buckle and twiddling his mittened hand, he said, 'So have we'."

When the pun had been translated everybody laughed.

Like most others, the soldiers in the 93rd and the IR133 had a sombre reason to get together in No Man's Land – to bury dead soldiers who had been left lying after earlier fights. This was also the official reason why there was a truce, according to the 93rd's war diary: "The Germans asked for leave to bury ten dead. This was granted." There is nothing in the diary about hundreds of soldiers milling around out in the field. It seems the keeper of the diary thought it would be unwise to tell the whole truth to future readers higher up in the staff.

At four o'clock in the afternoon soldiers on both sides were called in with signals from whistles. But it was not only dusk that forced them to come back. Johannes Niemann wrote that the commander of the battalion came to the front. His staff had had a report from the artillery, whose observers had watched the truce in their binoculars. "First he stood and looked helplessly at what

INTELLIGENCE SUMMARY.

(Erase heading not required.)

Hour, Date, Place	Summary of Events and Information	Re
22nd Dec. 6·30p·m	Quiet Day. Lieut BOYD with patrol went through German advanced wire and discovered Germans putting up wire entanglement.	
9 a.m	Conference at Batt Hd Qrs over projected enterprise & German trenches. This was cancelled by 6th Division order.	
23rd Dec	Germans heard moving transport from West to East	
10 p.m	2nd Lieut BANNIER arrived with 34 men.	
24th Dec	Work carried out in communication trenches. A new one made from C Coys line. Brig Gen'l CONGREVE 16th Inf Bde visited trenches before taking over	
25th Dec	Very quiet day. Germans came out of their trenches unarmed in afternoon, and were seen to belong to 133rd and 134th Regiments. The position was reconnoitred by Lieut ANDERSON. The Germans asked for leave to bury 10 dead. This was granted.	
26th 11 a.m	A few shells were fired at and in rear of our trenches, one going through the house used as an orderly room.	
5 p.m	Battalion relieved by Sherwood Foresters, the 19th Brigade going into Divisional Reserve at ARMENTIÈRES.	

The entry for 25 December in the 93rd's war diary does not mention
that hundreds of soldiers were out in No Man's Land. It just says that
the Germans wanted to bury ten soldiers, which was granted, and that
Lieutenant Anderson took the chance to reconnoitre the enemy position.

was going on," wrote Johannes Niemann, "until he suddenly
started shouting that this state of peace must be broken off."

Graham Hutchison, one of the officers in the 93rd wrote:
"We parted saying, 'Tomorrow it is war'." But this was not quite
true. According to Johannes Niemann the soldiers had made a
silent agreement not to start shooting until after New Year. "We

honoured this agreement and so did they over there. The staffs higher up might or might not have been aware of it." But at New Year the 93rd was no longer in the trenches. They were celebrating in Armantières. Their successors in the trenches between Houplines and Frelinghien kept the spirit of Christmas alive for another few days.

The 93rd left the trenches on Boxing Day, when the whole of 19th Brigade was given a rest and was in reserve for six days. Frank Collier wrote that they stayed in homes in Armentières, with people "who made us very welcome and as comfortable as possible." The news about the Christmas Truce had spread and there were those who were not pleased. Some French women stood in their doors and spat at the soldiers when they came marching from the trenches, a soldier in one of the other battalions in the brigade wrote. The ladies shouted: "You boko kamerade Allemagne!", the soldier noted. The soldiers answered with their worst curses.

The Match

ALBERT AND JIMMY

Nobody's home ground

This story ends in a field that lies on both sides of road D945 that runs between Houplines and Frelinghien in northern France (see map on page 134). Somewhere out there is the pitch where Saxons and Scots played football in No Man's Land on Christmas Day 1914.

Just west of the road, near the road that leads north to Ypres, is the place where there was a ruined farm. I believe that it was in the basement of this ruined house that some of the 93rd's officers had their command post, their straw beds and their dining table, where they had their Christmas dinner. The Germans named this ruin "Ferme la Moutarderie" and Johannes Niemann wrote this name in the map in his book. Today there is nothing left of the ruin. Where it was is now a field and when I was there in November 2013 the field was ploughed. It was not possible to walk out on the muddy, sucking earth on the field and I understood why some soldiers in the trenches did not dare wear their boots on their feet but wore them tied together around their necks.

This is where Ferme la Moutarderie was situated. The British trench was where the road is now. The German trenches were near the naked trees on the other side of the field. (Kristofer Sandberg)

The trench that ran close to the ruin of the farm is now under the D945 and a smaller side road. To the east are the fields that became No Man's Land when British and German soldiers dug their trenches in the autumn of 1914. The other way around, to the northwest, the river Lys and the border with Belgium is a third of a mile away. The distance along the trench line to the border is about two thirds of a mile.

From the southeast, from the direction to Lille, runs a road that is not exactly full of bends, but still not straight, which tells you that is it not new. There are many houses along the road, which also tell about its age. On Johannes Niemann's map this road is slightly highlighted, so perhaps it was a main road from Lille. It had a Y-junction from where one branch turned north to Frelinghien and the other turned west towards Houplines. The Houplines branch was left when D945 was built and it joins the new road in a roundabout. But the Frelinghien branch was degraded to a track across the field. It is still there with much of its asphalt intact. This stump of road runs over what was No Man's Land and it points right at where the ruined farm was. The German trench line ran some 100 yards west of the Y-junction. Right behind the German trenches there are now a few trees, whose branches, naked in November, are easily recognizable. The trees form a landmark that makes it possible to see from the place of the ruin where the German trenches were on the big flat field. The distance from the ruin to the trees is just over 400 yards, but straight to the east and to the northeast the German trenches were closer.

There is a picture of the field, taken from the air on 20 March 1916. The lines of trenches look like what Johannes Niemann drew in his map in his book (See map on page 134). The ruined farm protrudes like a nose from the British line. There are only a few shell holes in No Man's Land.

When I was out in these fields there was rain that seemed to just float around in the air. The ground was muddy and it seemed to be saturated with water. But on Christmas Day 1914 it was frozen and hard. I thought about the football players. How lucky they were with the weather!

I have found 29 accounts of German and British soldiers

The old road from Frelinghien towards Lille crossed No Man's Land. Somewhere in this field Scots and Saxons played football on Christmas Day. The German trenches were near the naked trees at the other side of the field. In another direction, to the left, they were closer.
(Kristofer Sandberg)

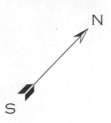

This photograph, taken on 20 March 1916, shows that there were no shell holes in the football field that would have made it difficult to play. The ground in No Man's Land was still almost untouched.

Ferme la Moutarderie protrudes like a nose from the British line of trenches, to the left. See also the map on page 134. (Imperial War Museum)

playing football between the trenches during the Christmas Truce. It is possible that some of these accounts are about the same incident. Most of them are about play or kickabouts with real balls. In one story the soldiers played with a tin, in another they had a football they had made then and there, possibly it was a sandbag stuffed with straw.

Football was the soldiers' favourite game on both sides. Franz von Kotsch, who was the commander of IR133 in the beginning of the war, wrote in his book about the regiment that one duty of the support behind the frontline was to organize football for the soldiers when they came out of the trenches. On the British side soldiers were said to be playing all the time. *The Daily Mirror* invited readers to send money for footballs to be sent to the front. In the history of the war published by *The Times* is a report of the fighting on the river Aisne in September 1914. The soldiers had come out of the trenches and they had slept in caves dug into a bank "and after a 'wash and brush up' someone will produce a football and they will be running about and playing football as if there weren't any Germans, or any trenches or any night-attacks on the Aisne."

James Jack wrote in late December about the soldiers of his company:

"Games, mainly football, in the afternoons keep them fit and cheery ...however tired the rascals may be for parades they have always energy enough for football..."

Douglas Haig, commander of the British First Army in the summer of 1915, thought that there was too much football. He wrote about a serious issue, namely soldiers falling asleep when they were on guard, which carried the death penalty.

"Men should rest during the day when they know they will be on sentry duty at night. Instead of resting they run about and play football."

And as for the 93rd, Aidan Liddell described a normal afternoon when not in contact with the enemy. There were work parties or training and sometimes games, usually football.

During the Christmas Truce both British and German soldiers had the idea to let a football match decide the outcome of the war. A British soldier said many years later: "Had just one of these Big Mouths [he referred to his lieutenant colonel, who had interrupted a game] gathered together ten thousand footballs, what a happy solution that would have been, without bloodshed."

A German 20-year-old student of medicine, who had studied in England and France, said that he would rather have a game of football than this, the war. And a German had the idea to settle the war with football or mudslinging.

Four of the accounts of matches or kickabouts are about the game between IR133 from Zwickau in Saxony and the 93rd from Fort George in Scotland. This match is the best documented of those mentioned in books and other sources. Gefreiter Albert Schmidt and Sergeant Jimmy Coyle are not mentioned, so I cannot say they took part. But it is more than a fascinating speculation that they played; it is a distinct possibility.

If so, Jimmy, as captain of the battalion team, must have been a leader also in this match. He was an ex-professional and possibly the strongest player on the pitch. Albert had not played at that level. He was inside right in the third team at home, a player who was never cheered by a large crowd but who still played because football had become a "necessity of life", as the author of the club history wrote later.

During an hour or so they were footballers, not soldiers.

It is Johannes Niemann who has given the most detailed account of the match. First he spoke about it in a BBC film before Christmas 1968. In the following year he wrote about it, with new details, in his book. In the film he said:

"Suddenly a Tommie came with a football, kicking and making fun and then [there] became a football match."

I had the opportunity to write to Pat O'Brien, a member of the team that worked on the BBC film in 1968. She gave me valuable information. She told me that it was certainly the BBC who contacted Johannes Niemann, probably with the help of a researcher. So it was not Johannes Niemann who came to the BBC to tell his story. Then Mrs O'Brien wrote:

"I remember him as a nice, stolid man of integrity, but without much sense of humour. I would say he was a trustworthy source."

This is what Johannes Niemann said about the football game:

"The Saxon and Scottish soldiers were out in the field between the trenches on Christmas Day. They talked and exchanged souvenirs. They hunted hares. They played football."

"We marked our goal with our caps. Tommies did also."

"There was a match according to the rules but the play was not pretty because the ground was frozen."

No, play probably was not pretty with heavy boots and clumsy clothes. But the pitch seems to have been not too bad in the circumstances. James Jack wrote in December that No Man's Land was a "level stretch of rank grass." This is confirmed by the aerial photograph from 1916. And the frozen ground must have made it less difficult to play. If the weather had been warm it would have been slippery also on the untouched grass, which I noticed when I was out in fields nearby around Christmas 2012.

One of the Saxon soldiers had a camera. The players arranged themselves for a proper football picture with both teams, each Saxon standing between two Scots and vice versa.

"The ball in the middle," wrote Johannes Niemann.

He has also given the result of the match. But how shall I write the score-line? The home team is usually mentioned first but in this game there was no home team. I cannot imagine that any game at any time has been played on a more neutral ground. It was nobody's home ground. It was No Man's Land. So I write the score line with the winners first, Saxony 3 – Scotland 2. Or, as Johannes Niemann wrote it:

"The game ended 3:2 for Fritz."

And the picture? No, it has not come to the surface, not yet.

Johannes Niemann's story is supported by Hugo Klemm, an officer in the regimental staff. Johannes Niemann quotes him in his book, but not about football. However, in the book *Christmas Truce* Hugo Klemm tells about football: "Everywhere you looked the occupants from the trenches stood around talking to each other and even playing football."

The Saxons were eager to play football. When the young officer Ian Stewart met two Saxons out in No Man's Land on the evening of Christmas Eve, one of them gave him a picture of the IR133 football team. During the truce many soldiers took out photographs of families or girlfriends. But among the Saxons there was one soldier who showed a picture of the team, rather than a picture of the dear ones at home.

On the British side there is only one known account of a match between the Saxons and the Scots. It was told by a sergeant in the 5th Battalion of the Scottish Rifles. This battalion had joined the 19th brigade in November. The sergeant wrote about the football match in a letter on Christmas Day, when he was on guard some 500 yards behind the front trenches. The letter was published in the *Glasgow News* on 2 January. The name of the sergeant is unfortunately not mentioned in the paper.

"There has been practically no shooting to-day, as some of our boys (the Argyll and Sutherland Highlanders) visited the Germans in their trenches, wished them a Merry Christmas, and arranged to have a truce for 24 hours. They also had a football match between the two lines of trenches and exchanged gifts of cigars and chocolates."

The sergeant also wrote that two of the Saxons had lived in Glasgow. He even mentioned where in the city they had lived. So even though he did not himself take part in the truce he had met someone who could talk about it in detail. That makes the sergeant's story about the truce and about the match more reliable.

Henry Hyslop, who was the battalion's second in command at Christmas, noted that the Saxons were interested in football. In his entry for Christmas Day he wrote: "They were very anxious to have a football match but this could not be arranged." Hyslop's entry indicates that the Scots were not unwilling to play, but practical problems seem to have prevented it.

Frank Collier, a soldier in A Company, wrote in the regimental magazine in 1965 that some Scots in the neighbouring platoon made a ball out of paper, rags and string and that they went on like

This picture shows the football team of the IR133 before the war. A Saxon soldier gave it to the Scottish officer Ian Stewart when they met in No Man's Land in the evening of Christmas Eve. In return Ian Stewart gave the Saxon a tin of meat. (From the book *Christmas Truce*)

mad until the ball fell to pieces after some twenty minutes. But it was no match and the Germans did not join. Three other Scots wrote about the Christmas Truce in letters or diaries without mentioning football: the machine gun officer Aidan Liddell, the officer Graham Hutchison and Doctor Frederick Chandler.

We have the following sources: two German soldiers who were out in No Man's Land, one of them (Niemann) wrote and said on TV that there was a match, the other (Klemm) said that there was football. A British soldier (the sergeant) wrote that there was a match, but he cannot have seen it. A British soldier

(Collier) wrote that some Scots had a homemade ball. A British soldier (Hyslop) wrote that a match could not be arranged. Two British soldiers and the Doctor (Liddell, Hutchison and Chandler) did not mention football.

Here I would like to add what a soldier in another unit has said about football. He was sure there was no football in No Man's Land because the ground was so churned up and because there were so many ditches and wire entanglements. But that is not what No Man's Land looked like between the Saxons and the Scots according to the officer James Jack, which we can also see on the aerial photograph from 1916.

So, was there a match between Saxons and Scots in No Man's Land on Christmas Day?

I believe there was a match. Johannes Niemann said on BBC that there was a match and he later wrote about it in his book. Hugo Klemm told about football. I do not think they invented such a story. Henry Hyslop wrote that it was not possible to arrange a game, as the Saxons wanted. I think that is right, but I think he meant a proper match with eleven players in each team, a referee and linesmen. There are several accounts of suggestions for such games during the truce, but they could not be realized. One reason probably was that the weather became mild and the mud of Flanders became mud again. A British officer has said that he was ordered to fill in shell holes in No Man's Land, prepare a pitch and ask the Germans for a game. He was so angry that he threw away the slip of paper with the order and there was no match.

I believe that the match between the Saxons and the Scots was a match like the matches I played, and surely many readers played, when we were at school. Of course we had no linesmen, we did not even have lines. We threw our bags, caps and clothes in little heaps to mark goals. We made up teams and then we played until the bell rang. That is how I think the soldiers played on Christmas Day. Thanks to football they were no longer soldiers, they were boys and they could play.

I cannot say why none of the Scots who were out there between the trenches wrote about a match. The reason could be that they found kicking a ball nothing to write about. It was just natural. The soldiers played all the time. Or, the reason could be that they did not see everything that happened in the fields.

There is also another question: why would one of the Scots bring a football to the trenches? Why would a soldier, on top of the usual load of material and supplies, add a football to his pack?

I put this question to Rod MacKenzie, a historian at the Argyll and Sutherland Highlanders Museum in Stirling. Firstly, he said, a football was valuable. When a soldier went into the trenches he dared not leave his football behind in the billets. It could easily be stolen and the soldier did not know that he would return to the same place. So he took his ball with him. Secondly, the football was a memento, a link to the time before the war, like a family photograph or locks of hair from the children.

And then there is a third reason for a soldier to bring his ball into the trenches, something I myself find plausible. I think the ball was a talisman. The soldier who carried the ball had come through all the fights and all the days and nights in the trenches. The ball had been there. It brought luck.

So it was not surprising that there was a ball at hand when there appeared a chance to play. A British soldier wrote several years after the war that "the Germans came out of their protective holes, fetched a football and invited our boys out for a little game. Our boys joined them and together they quickly had great fun till they ...had to return to their posts." Another British soldier wrote that "the ball appeared from somewhere ...it came from their side." Then started a giant kick-about with several hundred soldiers taking part. Yet another soldier wrote: "We had a football out in front of the trenches and asked the Germans to send a team to play us..." The German officer Kurt Zehmisch wrote in his diary about Christmas Day: "Soon a couple of Englishmen had got a football from their trenches and there was an intense match... Towards the evening the officers asked if we could arrange a big match for next day", but the Germans could not take part because they were being relieved and would leave the front trenches.

When Johannes Niemann described the football match in the BBC film and in his book he added something. He wrote that the Germans looked wide-eyed at the Scots as they chased the ball. They had never before seen soldiers in skirts.

"Our soldiers soon saw that the Scots wore no underpants under their skirts, so that their bottoms were clearly visible when their skirts fluttered. This amused us and at first we could not believe it before they told us [about how kilts are worn]," he wrote in his book. In the film he added: "That was the stuff to give the troops."

And then he turned around with his bottom towards the camera and let his coat flutter.

I do not know if footballers at that time exchanged shirts after a match. For Albert and Jimmy this cannot have been tempting.

None of them would have wanted the other's dirty and probably smelly and lousy shirt. But I like to think that they wanted to give each other something before they parted. Perhaps they pulled buttons from their uniforms and gave them as a memento of the match between the trenches.

Johannes Niemann explaining about the kilts, demonstrating with his coat tails. (From the 1968 BBC documentary "Christmas Day Passed Quietly")

And the war went on

A new truce in the mud

The weather became mild when the 93rd were relieved and left the trenches on Boxing Day. The soldiers walked back to Armentières, where the battalion celebrated New Year, played football and practised with the new hand grenades. The Saxons in IR133 remained in the trenches and had a quiet week until New Year. Both sides could use the truce to repair and build better trenches. The soldiers could work in the open without being shot at by the enemy. They took advantage of the truce and they prepared to go on fighting.

Both sides gave a salute when 1914 gave way to 1915. This was also the signal that they had resumed the war, Johannes Niemann wrote.

But the British and the Germans now had to spend more time defending themselves against rain and mud. When the 93rd went out to the front again on 2 January they came to trenches where water was up to their knees. Four soldiers lost their boots on their way to the front. One man sank into a mud hole and it took six men to get him out, wrote Aidan Liddell.

The weather got worse. The water rose. On 6 January the war diary noted that the water level had risen one foot since four days earlier.

Frank Collier wrote that the water in his trench was over his ankles when they came. Then the water rose to his waist on 7 January. "By this time all our rifles were absolutely unfit for use, mud being all through the mechanism of the body.

The fight against mud continued in January 1915. The picture shows soldiers in the 93rd who built breastworks, standing on the ground, instead of digging trenches. It was the same for the Germans. Their position was by the trees in the background. While the soldiers worked they stopped shooting at each other. (Imperial War Museum, Q56199)

Everything we were not actually wearing was well underneath the mud and water." But all this water did not come from above. "[It] was pumped into our trenches by the enemy, which plan was rendered easier owing to a ditch running at a slight gradient from their trench to ours."

It was not possible to walk in the communication trenches that led to the front trenches. The soldiers must expose themselves to German snipers when they moved from one place to another. But, the war diary noted, "as the enemy was evidently as badly off only two casualties (one killed, one wounded) were suffered." Men were killed or wounded every other day also during this time when the soldiers were fully occupied bailing water and mud with little time to spare for organizing any killing. Many soldiers were also sick.

To dig was very difficult or impossible. The mud stuck to the spades. One company abandoned its trench and dug a new one right behind. They found they were digging through an old latrine and they found dead soldiers. Finally both sides gave up. Instead of digging they started building breastworks, which were walls that stood on the ground. This was dangerous because the soldiers had no protection when they worked. Aidan Liddell wrote that he ordered his machine guns to fire at German soldiers who carried timber "so there's been no more wood carrying since."

The soldiers started building breastworks (fortifications) during the nights, but soon both the Scots and the Germans opposite worked also at daytime without trying to kill the enemies at the other side of the field. The men on both sides waved at each other. Aidan Liddell saw a German officer who sat

The Scots in the 93rd fought their enemies with spades and hand grenades. And there was also room for an accordion when the soldiers marched out to this seemingly very dry position.
(Argyll and Sutherland Highlanders)

on a chair directing the work. And Doctor Frederick Chandler wrote:

"The ground was a sticky bog in places and a turbid lake in others. These breastworks could never have been made at all, except through a tacit agreement between our men and the Germans ...In some places this work was done within fifteen or

In the fight against lice the soldiers tried to keep clean as best they could.
They usually went for weeks and even months without a bath.
(Argyll and Sutherland Highlanders)

twenty yards of each other, and in one part souvenirs were freely exchanged. We could walk right up to the German line and say 'Good morning' to the German officers sitting on their parapet."

After the Christmas Truce, this was the mud truce. It was not only live and let live, but build and let build.

The 93rd stayed in this position for 11 days. "In order to get out of the trench we were assisted with ropes," wrote Frank Collier. "At this time numerous cases of frostbit feet were being sent home but my feet altho' extremely painful refused to swell." When Frank Collier's company came out of the trenches the soldiers rested in a farm where they found straw to sleep on. "We could not sleep the first night for excessive heat in our feet."

Albert Schmidt's Regiment IR133 also stayed in the same area and must have struggled against the mud in the same way. Parts of the regiment were sometimes sent out as reinforcements. Albert Schmidt's company was part of a force that was sent some 12 miles to the south in March. This force lost 366 of its 859 soldiers during three days of fighting. In June the regiment was sent to near this place to take over a section of trenches. The defences consisted mostly of shell holes and shallow trenches that had been damaged by British grenades. When the Saxons started building new defences they made the same terrible discoveries that the Scots had made earlier.

"It was too bad to see that when we dug we came upon fallen soldiers again and again," Johannes Niemann wrote.

◉ ALBERT AND JIMMY ◉

Two destinies in the Great War

In the summer of 1916 IR133 was sent to the area around the river Somme, where British and French forces had started an attack that arguably became the worst catastrophe during the whole war. It is called the Battle of the Somme. Also on the

Food in the trenches was monotonous, mostly tinned meat stew and army biscuits. Many soldiers had more tasty food sent from home.
(Argyll and Sutherland Highlanders)

German side casualties were terrible. During this fight Albert Schmidt was killed.

The regiment was at the front, facing northwest, a few miles north of the Somme. During 17 and 18 August the regiment on IR133's left side had been forced to withdraw, but IR133 managed to stay in their position. During the night between 20 and 21 August soldiers from Australia attacked the Saxons and managed to get into their defences. The First Battalion of IR133, which was held in reserve just behind the front, made a counter attack. Albert Schmidt was killed on 20 August.

His grave is in the German war cemetery in a nearby village, Villers-au-Flos. I visited his grave in December 2012. Albert Schmidt shares a cross with another soldier. When I was there it was raining and the grey clouds gave the graves and the monument on the cemetery a darker impression than if the sun had been out. But the black crosses on this German cemetery are different from the white stones on other nations' burial places.

The 93rd also took part in the Battle of the Somme – Six hundred and seventy-five of its soldiers were killed or wounded or reported missing.

A little over two years later, in September 1918, the 93rd walked to the front near Villers-Guislain, some 25 miles east of the place where Albert Schmidt was killed. This is where Jimmy Coyle distinguished himself and was awarded the Military Medal.

The British took Villers-Guislain from the Germans in April 1917, when the Germans retired to newly built defences after the Battle of the Somme the year before. Then the Germans recaptured Villers-Guislain in their last effort to win the war in the spring of 1918. But in the autumn the Germans were again

Albert Schmidt's grave is at the German war cemetery in
Villers-au-Flos in France. (Pehr Thermaenius)

retreating and the war was to be over in a few months. But the
soldiers did not know this so the fighting went on as before.

In the evening of 19 September 1918, the 93rd took over
trenches that British soldiers had taken the day before. The Scots
had orders to press on and to drive the Germans out of trenches
further on. This fight lasted three days. The Scots managed to
get into the German trenches a few times, but were driven back.
After the three days of fighting they were back where they started,
so looking at the situation in the war nothing had happened.
But 141 soldiers in the 93rd had been killed or wounded and

other soldiers were missing or had been taken prisoners. On 30 September the battalion could at last move forward after the Germans had abandoned their positions, because other German forces on their sides were forced to retreat.

One of the dangerous situations for the 93rd during this three-day fight arose at midday on 23 September. The Germans had made a counter attack and driven the 93rd so far back that they were behind the position that they had taken over on 19 September. The Scots had almost no ammunition left and no hand grenades. The war diary describes what happened:

"To meet this situation, emergency parties consisting of Headquarter servants, Pioneers, etc. were despatched on two repeated and successive journeys to the front line. They were shortly followed by parties from Brigade Headquarters with ample supplies."

What Jimmy Coyle probably did to qualify for his Military Medal was to get up to the front through the German fire with ammunition for the fighting soldiers.

IR133 fought for the last time in the war on 17 October 1918 near Wassigny in northern France. Three German regiments fought together. When they went into the war their combined strength was close to 10,000 men. Now they had shrunk to the same strength as one battalion, fewer than 1,000 men, Johannes Niemann wrote. Still, these regiments had been reinforced with thousands of men during the war.

The regiment's first commander in the war, Franz von Kotsch, wrote in his book about IR133: "From the men, who during the war passed through the rolls of many infantry regiments, you could almost have formed a division [that usually consisted of four regiments]."

After the armistice on 11 November the IR133 marched back into Germany. Johannes Niemann wrote that the soldiers were in good spirits and that the band played the regimental march when they passed through villages and towns. From Karlsruhe they travelled by train and they came back to Zwickau on 26 November. People were out in the streets to give them a warm welcome.

In a three volume work titled *Sachsen in grösser Zeit*, published during 1919–1920, is a table that gives the regiment's losses during the war. Some 2,835 soldiers in IR133 were killed. When missing soldiers are added the total is 3,696. The number of wounded soldiers was 7,711. This history of the war also sums up how all Saxony was affected. Out of 5 million inhabitants:

One million were men of military age of which 750,000 were in the war. Of these, 213,000 were killed, 334,000 wounded and 42,000 taken prisoner (including my estimate of how many of the missing soldiers were in these categories). The sum of all these is 78 per cent of those who served in the war.

The 93rd fought for the last time in the war at the river Sambre on 4–7 November. This is 12 miles from Le Cateau in northern France where the battalion lost almost half of its soldiers in August 1914. It is also not quite 20 miles north of Wassigny, where IR133 fought for the last time. During the 93rd's last fight five soldiers were killed and 63 were wounded. The regimental history says inhabitants showed their joy to have been liberated after four years "in the most touching and effusive manner."

The battalion spent the winter and the spring in France demobilizing and training. The soldiers left France from Le Havre and came to Stirling on 22 May 1919. The regimental history gives the number of soldiers in the battalion who were killed in the war as 1,238. Several thousand more men were wounded.

Jimmy Coyle was greeted by his daughter Doreen Agnes Norrie, now five years old, and by his wife Nellie. It was a fond reunion. Their second daughter was born nine months later, on Valentine's Day 14 February 1920. They named her Ruth Liddle.

Liddle. Was that a coincidence? No, I do not think it was.

Aidan Liddell, the 93rd's machine gun officer has contributed several quotes to my story. He left the 93rd when he became ill in early 1915. Then he joined the Royal Flying Corps, which was the name of the air force. On 31 July 1915 his aeroplane was hit by bullets from an enemy plane on the German side of the front. Aidan Liddell was badly wounded in his leg and fainted. He woke up and managed to fly the damaged aircraft across the front, and land, thus saving himself and his observer. For this he was awarded the Victoria Cross, the highest British decoration for valour.

All this was extensively reported in the newspapers, with sensationally good news photographs. In one picture Aidan Liddell is seen smiling at the camera and waving as he is carried from his aircraft on a stretcher. But a short time after that he died. I think that Jimmy and Nellie Coyle gave their daughter the second name Liddle in memory of the officer who Jimmy had worked with in France and Flanders.

There are two pictures of Jimmy Coyle in the Argyll and Sutherland Highlanders' Museum in Stirling in Scotland. The first is a picture of the 93rd's football team for the season 1911–1912. Jimmy, who had perhaps recently played professional football at the time when the picture was taken, is smiling and seems radiating self-confidence. The other picture is a formal portrait from the time after the war. Jimmy is in uniform and he wears his medals. The pictures are different: one with his teammates, the other formal in uniform. Still I think I can see that he has changed. In the post-war picture his experiences from the war seem to burden him.

But from the little I know about him I think he came through the war better than many others who survived. He was promoted to company sergeant major, the highest rank of a non-commissioned officer. He had his family. And he still played football.

Jimmy Coyle left the army in 1926 after serving for 21 years. He was then 39 years old. His pension was increased in recognition of his long service and good conduct.

Jimmy Coyle wore his Military Medal when he was photographed after the war. The picture was published and the caption said: "All ranks wish him long life and health to wear his coveted decoration."
(Argyll and Sutherland Highlanders)

What if...

There was more to the truce than presents and football

Murdoch McKenzie Wood was a lieutenant during the war in the 6th Battalion of the Gordon Highlanders, the battalion that took part in the mass funeral between the trenches on Christmas Day. He was wounded in 1915 and then served in Britain. After the war he was a member of parliament for a constituency in Scotland. In a debate in parliament in 1930 about the rights of conscientious objectors he spoke about the Christmas Truce.

"If we had been left to ourselves there would never have been another shot fired," he said.

He was one of few soldiers in the truce who thought like that. A German officer clasped his hands, gazed at the sky and said: "My God, why cannot we have peace and let us all go home!"

But most other soldiers were intent on enjoying the truce while it lasted, take the opportunity to repair trenches, try to find out as much as possible about the enemy and then continue the war as before. This is how the officer and cartoonist Bruce Bairnsfather described it: "There was not an atom of hate that day and yet, on our side, not for a moment was the will to war and the will to beat them relaxed. It was just like the interval between rounds in a friendly boxing match."

There is one impossible question that comes up when you study the Christmas Truce: what would have happened if the soldiers had let the truce go on, if they had refused to start the war again, if officers who threatened to shoot those who refused to shoot had not been able to scare the soldiers into obedience. What if...?

To answer such questions is called writing contra factual history, which means that the author speculates about what could have been if things had turned out quite contrary to what actually happened. The historian Stanley Weintraub has written contra factually about what would have happened if the First World War had ended at Christmas 1914.

"[Then] one enters the fantasy world of alternative history. It is an intriguing and illuminating, yet dangerous place to visit."

The first thing that he mentions in his contrary history is that many people would have been saved from suffering if the war had ended on the evening of Christmas Eve. This is the only thing that is certain.

Then he takes a speculative trip round world politics: In Russia Bolshevism would have failed. Germany would have become a monarchy with a social democratic government, where Adolf Hitler would have become no more than a demobbed vice corporal who had found a job in the growing economy. Great Britain would have been able to maintain her empire a little longer. France would not have recaptured Alsace and Lorraine, which Germany had won in 1871, and French revanchism would continue to be a risk. Stanley Weintraub's speculative round then takes the reader into the wide world, to the Middle East, Africa, Asia and America. He writes about how the soldiers in the Christmas Truce could have influenced developments worldwide. Provided, that is, that the war had stopped then and there, which however did not happen.

But there is another speculation, which is closely connected with reality and which is always interesting. It is about conflict resolution and mediation. Was there a chance to mediate when, as Johannes Niemann put it, "peace had broken out"? It is not known that anyone actually took such an initiative in 1914. There did not seem to exist any opening for negotiations. The German armies had occupied almost all of Belgium and a large part of France. But I wonder how present day mediators would have tackled a request to make an effort to solve the conflict. How would they have used mediators' experiences and the advances of conflict research over the one hundred years since 1914?

I had the opportunity to put the question to Peter Wallensteen, professor of Peace and Conflict Research at Uppsala University in Sweden and University of Notre Dame in Indiana, USA: "Suppose you had received a telephone call in the evening of Christmas Eve in 1914, that somebody had said: 'The war has stopped, come and help us take this chance to have peace.' What would you have done?"

"I have had such a call," Peter Wallensteen answered.

It was in January 1990. The call came from a group of academics who tried to make peace on the island of Bougainville in Papua New Guinea, where government forces were fighting against a guerrilla that wanted to make the island independent.

What had triggered the conflict were protests against the management of a very profitable copper mine on the island.

"We read your article. We think it is relevant. Can you come?" a representative for the peace group said in the telephone.

Peter Wallensteen had lectured on the article at a conference six months earlier. It is about making use of opportunities to mediate that appear when both sides in a conflict are blocked in a way that is detrimental to both of them. Technically this is called a hurting stalemate and this is what had happened on Bougainville.

The conflict on the island had been going on for several years and Peter Wallensteen knew about it. One group on the island wanted independence. But the government wanted to prevent Bougainville from separating from Papua New Guinea, which would probably lead to more breakaways. A military force with soldiers from other parts of the country tried to defeat the guerrillas, but failed.

The deadlock was bad for both sides. The guerrillas fought without gaining anything. The government wanted an end to the conflict, which was expensive. It was expensive to keep the military force on the island and there was no income from the mine. On top of that, the conflict gave Papua New Guinea a bad reputation. In this situation the group of academics had succeeded to persuade both the guerrillas and the government to agree to talk to a mediator from the outside.

Peter Wallensteen travelled to Bougainville and listened to both parties. The only thing they could agree to was that they wanted an end to the fighting. They disagreed about everything else.

"But when I started talking to them, I understood what was the most important."

For the guerrillas, self-government was more important than independence and the government was prepared to grant self-government to Bougainville as long as the island remained a part of Papua New Guinea. Both parties listened with interest when Peter Wallensteen told them about the status of the island province of Åland in Finland. Although Peter Wallensteen's task was not to discuss Bougainville's future status in the country, his reference to Åland still helped him to bring the parties to sign the armistice on 1 March 1990. When Peter Wallensteen on his way back from his last meeting with the guerrilla leader passed through a government roadblock, soldiers came forward to thank him: "Now we can go home," they said.

If Peter Wallensteen had had a telephone call on Christmas Eve in 1914, his experience from 1990 would have been useful. The situation on the Western Front was similar to the situation on Bougainville. The first resemblance was that time was short.

"These phone calls can come and then it is important to set off right away," Peter Wallensteen said when I visited him in Uppsala in the autumn of 2013.

Another important resemblance is that the deadlock in 1914 was bad for both parties. After the first months of mobile war, which was what the generals on both sides had planned for, the war had ground to a halt. The soldiers had dug trenches and none of the parties could make significant advances and hold on to them.

The Germans had not been able to follow their plan to march towards Paris and defeat France in September. And Germany's new plan had also failed. It was to take the French coast where German U-boats could have been based and well placed for attacks on British warships and freight ships.

France and Britain had also failed. They had not managed to stop the German armies and force them back into Germany.

And after five months of war on the Western Front some half a million soldiers had been killed and another one and quarter million had been wounded, taken prisoner or were missing. All over France, Britain, Belgium and Germany the war had caused suffering. So this was a hurting stalemate.

In an attempt to mediate in 1914 Peter Wallensteen would, as he did on Bougainville, have taken advantage of coming from outside, from a country that was not part of the conflict. And he would have turned to the Swedish Prime Minister Hjalmar Hammarskjöld, whose policy was to keep Sweden neutral. He was the father of Dag Hammarskjöld, who was to become general secretary of the United Nations. Hjalmar Hammarskjöld had experience of mediating. He had been involved when Norway and Sweden separated peacefully in 1905.

With the help of the Prime Minister Peter Wallensteen would have called a meeting with the warring countries' ambassadors to Stockholm. These were men of influence who had been sent out to the important embassies in Sweden. They would be given a message: "Here is an opportunity to stop the war. We have a plan. Please take it to your governments."

The plan would have been to first persuade the parties to make the soldiers' armistice official, perhaps to the Epiphany. Then Peter Wallensteen would have requested both sides to clarify their war aims, that is what the conflict really was about.

That is how he had dissected the conflict at Bougainville.

Peter Wallensteen would have taken advantage of the truce having happened during a Christian festival. So did the mediator George Mitchell in Northern Ireland in 1998, when he managed to broker an agreement between the political parties and the governments of Britain and Ireland on Good Friday. The name of that day in English, Good Friday, made the parties try harder to agree to the deal.

It is difficult to see how soft arguments like that can have an influence on hard decisions to make war, but this is well known, Peter Wallensteen said. Mediators trying to solve the present day conflict in Syria have tried to connect initiatives to religious festivals and to days that have a special significance.

Peter Wallensteen can list many difficulties that he would have met during an attempt to mediate in 1914. Russia, for example, would have feared that an armistice on the Western Front would allow Germany to send its forces to the Eastern front. That would have been just one of the knots that the mediator must untie. Peter Wallensteen then would have tried something unexpected.

"I would have tried something royal. England's Queen Victoria would have been an opener. I would have said, that this is what she would have done. There were several monarchs involved who were related to the Queen," Peter Wallensteen said.

Queen Victoria, who ruled Britain for 63 years, died in 1901. She was the British King George V's paternal grandmother and the German Emperor Wilhelm II's maternal grandmother. Victoria's son Edward (George's father) had been married to a sister of the Russian Tsar Nicholas II's mother. So George, Wilhelm and Nicholas were cousins. And Queen Victoria was also the maternal grandmother of Nicholas' wife Alexandra. This is why Peter Wallensteen would involve Queen Victoria, this would make the parties listen.

When Peter Wallensteen had persuaded the enemies to formalize the soldiers' Christmas Truce it would have been essential for him to get real negotiations started to solve the conflicts that had caused the war. He would still have been in a hurry. If the negotiations dragged on for too long there would have been the risk that one party, or all of them, would have lost patience. They would have concluded that it was better to break the armistice and that they would be able to better solve the conflict by defeating the enemy.

This is how the mediation at Bougainville failed after Peter Wallensteen had left for home. The real negotiations about the island's status in Papua New Guinea did not take off. In May 1990 the guerrillas took back their weapons, which they had given up in March and so the war started again. Of the island's 150,000 inhabitants an estimated 1,500 were killed. It took until 2001 before Bougainville had peace.

"They lost this opportunity. That is also an important lesson to be learnt from Bougainville," Peter Wallensteen said.

"It is not enough to put forward logical proposals or proposals that have proved effective in other conflicts. In each situation there are both those who want to keep the war going, believing that it can be won, and those who are open for peace initiatives. At Christmas 1914 there were too many who believed in a full victory."

"Peace initiatives from the other side can easily be taken as a sign that they suffer more than we do and it is just a matter of time before they capitulate. Such thoughts make it difficult for peace initiatives to get across."

In what way would the results of 100 years of conflict research have helped a mediator in 1914?

"Today we have systematic knowledge that did not exist then. There is an aversion to war that was not known in 1914, when it was regarded heroic to go out to fight. We have institutions, like the UN, with a mission to prevent war or broker peace. What we have today came after the First World War."

"We have better means of avoiding war today, but still there were 32 armed conflicts in 2012. Six of those were defined as wars, according to the Uppsala Conflict Data Program. It takes more to eliminate the curse of war, as set out in the UN charter."

Peter Wallensteen realizes how difficult it would have been to take advantage of the Christmas Truce to put an end to the war. Still he would have started working if he had been called in on Christmas Eve.

"You must take every opportunity. It is difficult to know what the chances of success are before you have tried. In too many conflicts actors have thought that nothing was possible and therefore they have not tried to make use of openings that they have seen."

In the autumn of 2013 I also had the opportunity to put my question – what would you have done? – to Therese Jönsson at The Folke Bernadotte Academy in Stockholm. At that time she was engaged in reconciliation in Kenya after the violence that broke out after the presidential election in 2007. She worked with the training of dialogue facilitators. Their task was to bring people together who had not sat down with each other for years.

On one occasion a facilitator invited 50 people, but 100 turned up.

I asked: How would you have taken on a request to mediate if the telephone had rung at Christmas night 1914?

Therese Jönsson first made it clear that the soldiers' truce opened ways for mediation, but that it would have taken more to reach a lasting peace.

"The soldiers are not parties to the conflict. They are the tools. Not even the generals are parties to the conflict. The parties are the rulers of the conflicting states. The basis for mediation is that the parties agree to it and they must take an active part in the process. If not, the mediator's solution of the conflict will be forced upon them and a forced solution usually does not last. The parties must be convinced that they 'own' the mediation process."

"Without the consent of the rulers it would not have been possible to get a negotiation going."

So it was a hopeless case?

"No, it was not necessarily a hopeless case. You cannot tell what position the rulers will take before they have been asked."

So Therese Jönsson would not have travelled to Flanders but to Berlin, Paris and London. Time was short, she could not spend days studying the conflict, so she would have needed assistance from someone who was familiar with the situation. She would also have needed help to get access to the leaders, at first in Berlin and London because it was mainly their soldiers who had stopped shooting at each other.

Then she would have needed luck, getting the timing right so that she could have put her proposals forward at the right moment. But this would have been mainly out of her control because she must act during the days while the truce lasted. The timing, however, seems not to have been so bad with the war ground to a halt and the terrible losses during the first months. Therese Jönsson would have sought support in the civilian communities. It would have been possible to get public support for a mediating initiative with so many messages going out about husbands, fathers or sons killed in the war.

And even if the soldiers were only the tools of the political leaders, the Christmas Truce would have given the mediators a chance. The fact was that the soldiers had stopped shooting, the war had stopped. This made an impression. The newspapers reported the truce with photographs from the front. People saw that this was real.

"I would have told the leaders, let us make this an official armistice, let us try to have a conversation. The war has ground to a halt, no one is on the offensive and none of you needs to break off any initiative. Let us try to start a dialogue. The soldiers can remain in readiness in the trenches, you have nothing to lose."

"I would also have reminded them about the costs of the war, both in human lives and money. If there were an armistice they would save both soldiers and ammunition. The opponents would make the same saves, but still."

Let us now suppose that Therese Jönsson had been able to persuade the parties to make a pause in the war to start a conversation. That would be the start of her real job.

To explain this she made a drawing of an onion, or one must think of two onions, one for each of the parties. In the center of the onions are the parties' needs. Outside of the needs are their interests. And outside of that, at the surface of the onions are the parties' positions. For a mediator to be successful she must find out what is at the centre of the onions, hidden by what they say they want (positions) and what they would like to achieve (interests). The mediator must understand what they really need. Therese Jönsson pretended to peel an onion. This is the way to do it, to peel off leaf after leaf until you get to the centre, to the needs of the parties.

Then the parties, with the help of the mediator, must find other means than war to satisfy their needs. The trick is to find solutions that satisfy the needs of both parties. There are examples of such successful mediations. One is the solution to the border conflict between Egypt and Israel in 1978. Israel's needs, at the centre of the onion, was to avoid the threat of Egyptian armed forces close to its border. Egypt's need was to keep its territory intact. The solution was to make the land along the border a demilitarized zone. This satisfied the needs of both parties.

The British historian Niall Ferguson has described what was in the centre of Britain's and Germany's onions in 1914.

The British foreign minister Edward Grey wrote after the war that the British could not accept a German victory in the war because that would have meant that Germany dominated the Continent. Britain was also morally bound to help France and legally bound to help Belgium. But most of this was on the outer leaves of the onion. Britain had no formal agreement with France and when it came to the formal guarantee of the neutrality of Belgium several members of the government were prepared to ignore it. What was most important, at the centre of the onion, was not to allow Germany to dominate the Continent. Germany made its aims public in the autumn, after the outbreak of war. In January 1915 the *Vanity Fair* magazine in USA carried an article on the war aims with a map that showed that Germany would take Belgium, north-eastern France and for a time occupy London and environs. Germany would also take the Baltic States from Russia. Austria-Hungary would take Poland, but the map did not cover the Balkans, so Germany's intentions there cannot be seen.

But Niall Ferguson points out that Germany made these war aims public only after Britain had become an enemy in the war. The days before Britain declared war on Germany on 4 August leaders in Germany had promised not to take any territory from either Belgium or France. There would not have been any German naval bases on the Channel coast. Surely, one of the German aims was to demand reparation from France that would prevent the country from rearming. There were also aims for colonies in Africa. But apart from this, several aims were low-keyed, for example allowing German businesses to compete on equal terms with French businesses in France and to create a European economical union. Germany would dominate this union, but its dominance would be industrial and financial, not military. This is strikingly similar to today's EU with rights for businesses to compete on equal terms in member countries and with Germany acting as the union's economic locomotive.

This was what was in the centre of the German onion. There seems to have been needs like survival, a prosperous economy and development.

So there would have been much for a mediator to discuss with the parties to help them find a common solution that satisfied the needs of both of them. First by asking "why" questions to find out what the conflict was really about, then by brainstorming together with the parties.

"Common solutions are generated by the process of mediation. They cannot be put forward by the mediator before the process has started," Therese Jönsson said.

"At the end of it everybody cannot be 100 per cent satisfied. But it is enough if the parties can get more out of mediation than they think they can win using violence, that is if the benefit of breaking off the war is greater than the risk. Furthermore, mediation often helps the parties to better understand each other's needs and to realize that in the long run it is better for oneself if the opponent's needs are also satisfied."

The conclusion is: it would not have been hopeless. A mediator could have been successful or could at least have been given a chance to have a chance. There was more to the Christmas Truce than exchanging Christmas presents and playing football.

100 years later

Lest we forget

The First World War still influences how we think and speak and write.

The head of a British bank said, ahead of a major change: "I would like to be in the trenches with my people." A newspaper reported that asset managers compete for pension funds in a "trench war". Another newspaper article was about Russia "conducting a diplomatic trench war on all fronts."

It is dangerous to speak and write in this way. It may be just playing with words, but it is a dangerous game because it makes us lose contact with the real meaning of the word trench. The competition for pension funds is not like trench warfare. The participants need not stand with wet boots in cold mud and they do not risk being killed by the opponents in the next moment.

I wrote in a newspaper about Stockholm's first fenced off parking lot for wrongly parked cars, which were towed away from the streets. It had a steel fence and I wrote that this was a concentration camp for cars. Next day another journalist in the office told me that the fenced off parking lot was not like a concentration camp. No one was kept prisoner there and no one was murdered. I was ashamed and made up my mind to be careful with war words. But still, when my grandchildren tell me they have learnt to bike or to write their names I might answer "Kanon!" This is the Swedish word for a big gun and it is a stupid way of saying "Brilliant!" or "Well done!" When this happens I bite my tongue and promise myself to think before I speak.

I wish this would spread, that everybody promises themselves to think before they speak or write. I wish that a newspaper, that reported on the Swedish team in the women's European football championship in 2013, had not written: "Iceland's game plan: A boring battleground." I wish that a columnist had not written: "Anyone who have opened a newspaper this week have noted at least two journalistic civil wars going on, which make the conflict in Syria look both easy to understand and easy to solve."

I also wish that symbols that have something to do with war were used only on occasions that has something to do with war. Barrack Obama's visit to Sweden in the autumn of 2013 was not about war. Still he was welcomed by a military band. I wish that the government had sent a group from the Stockholm Philharmonic Orchestra to greet him. This would have shown to the world what Sweden wants, just like when the cabinet the next day sent all its women ministers to the airport to bade the president farewell.

This is also why I wish that kings and princes do not wear their uniforms when they are not on military duties. Why do they wear military clothes when they or their children get married? Surely, those are celebrations when they and the people cheering outside their castles do not want to think of war.

The war 1914–1918, and especially the war on the Western Front clearly demonstrates what war is about. If it had not been so terrible one could even say that it was a pedagogic war. By reading what the people who were in the war tell us about it we can avoid being blunted and we learn to use the war words thoughtfully. That is why it is important to study the First World War.

Acknowledgements
Thanks

During a few years I have been visiting archives and libraries in my search for information about Albert Schmidt and Jimmy Coyle. In all of those places people have helped me and have also encouraged me in my work.

Two of these helpers gave me the most valuable leads. In Stadtarchiv Zwickau Jürgen Schünzel showed me the football club's 25-year history from 1927. This is where I found Albert Schmidt. In the regimental museum of the Argyll and Sutherland Highlanders at Stirling Castle Rod MacKenzie showed me the two pictures of Jimmy Coyle.

Manfred Beyer in Dresden wrote back when I sent out emails to anybody I could find who was connected with military history in Saxony. He is an active member of Arbeitskreis Sächsische Militärgeschichte. From then on he has helped me. He has shared documents and pictures from his archive and he has answered many questions. He also guided me in Sächsisches Staatsarchiv in Dresden. Then in Zwickau I was guided by Lorenz Zentgraf, who answered questions and showed his archive. Local historian Norbert Peschke has helped me in the same way. Christoph Meister in Germany helped me with the language.

When I first came to the museum in Stirling it was Archie Wilson who answered my questions and showed me documents. When I came next time to start working Rod MacKenzie had laid a table for me with books and diaries. Then he guided me in the museum archive, where he seems to know every shelf without the help of the computer. In the museum in Stirling I was lucky to share a table with Tom Greenshields, who knows everything that I need to know. He read my text and gave me much to think about. In Stirling is also my friend Scott Patrick. He too has read my text and helped me with the language and many other things.

Robert Morris guided me on the Edinburgh of the early 20th century, which also helped me get more out of the material laid in front of me in the National Library of Scotland. In Mitchell Library in Glasgow I was shown the small newspaper article about the sergeant who wrote about football between the Scots and the Saxons. And in the database of the Scottish Football Museum I was shown the entry about Jimmy Coyle's contract with Albion Rovers. Richard Gray helped me get to the Airdrie Library and Allan MacKenzie helped me find what the local newspapers wrote about Jimmy Coyle's matches.

Jesper Ericsson works in the museum of the Gordon Highlanders in Aberdeen. He answered my questions fully and quickly. Alan Weeks answered questions about the soldiers' food. I have learnt much from contributors to the websites *The Long Long Trail* and *Great War Forum*. There I got in touch with Colin Taylor, who looked up documents in the National Archives. When I came there myself they patiently answered my beginner's questions. I have visited the Imperial War Museum many times and had the privilege of studying their material in the reading room, the picture library and the film archive.

Tasmin Bacchus kindly let me use her grandfather E.R.P.

Berryman's drawings. In the archives of the In Flanders Fields Museum in Ypres, Pieter Trogh had prepared material for me. Together with Dominiek Dendooven he was always ready to help me, then as well as later. Kristin de Meyre is a guide in Ypres. Thanks to her I made good use of my days in Flanders. When I returned in the autumn of 2013 photographer Kristofer Sandberg came along to take pictures of the football field.

In Stockholm I have visited the library of the Army Museum and the Anna Lindh Library. Their advice saved me much time and I could study material that I had earlier just had time to leaf through during short days in London. The mediators Therese Jönsson and Peter Wallensteen took time to speculate how they could have used the Christmas Truce to end the war. Johnny Carlsson at the Artillery Museum in Kristianstad answered questions and gave me background material. I happened to meet the knowledgeable Hans Aili on the Internet. He read my text and suggested valuable improvements.

All of you gave me what I needed to be able to make my idea real. Thank you.

After my book was published in Sweden by Atlantis Bokförlag I wrote to some 70 publishers and literary agents in the UK. No one dared take on my story until I was introduced to Ryan Gearing and Uniform Press. He took the risk. I say "Thank You", but the words are too small.

Please write to me

I ask readers, who have information about the Christmas Truce and especially about those who played football, to write to me. My email address is: footballinnomansland@gmail.com.

My sources

Many sources are also mentioned in the text.

THE ROAD TO A FIELD IN FLANDERS

I have calculated casualties and reinforcements for the IR133 from the regiment's reports to the 40th Division. They are in Sächsisches Staatsarchiv in Dresden. Some of these reports I could not understand, some cannot be read because they are bound into the spine of the pack of documents. My figures, therefore, are incomplete. As for the 93rd I have not found any systematic reporting of casualties for 1914. I have used information from the war diaries of the 93rd and the 19th Brigade and several other sources. The war diaries are in the National Archives in London. I have compared information from these sources and used the most probable figures. Information about reinforcements come from the battalion's war diary and seems to be complete.

Information about Albert Schmidt comes from lists of soldiers who were recommended for a medal and awarded medals, held by Sächsisches Staatsarchiv, the football club's 25-year history *25 Jahre Fussballclub 02 Zwickau, 1902–1927* and *Volksbund Deutsche Kriegsgräberfürsorge.* (The football club changed its name

in the 1920s when Schedewitz became a part of Zwickau.) Information about Jimmy Coyle also came from battalion documents and the diary of Henry Hyslop, all held by the museum of the Argyll and Sutherland Highlanders in Stirling. Records of his football career are in the Scottish Football Museum and in Airdrie Library.

THE BOYS FROM SCHEDEWITZ

Information about Schedewitz and Zwickau came from Stadtarchiv Zwickau, military historian Lorenz Zentgraf and local historian Norbert Peschke and from their book *Die Garnison Zwickau* (2006). Information about football comes from Peschke's book *100 Jahre Fussball in der Zwickauer Region* (2006).

A VANMAN IN EDINBURGH

Information about Jimmy Coyle's family is in the regimental records. Professor Robert Morris told me about living conditions in Edinburgh. I have read parts of *The Making of Hibernian* by Alan Lugton (1995).

THE PLAYERS WHO EARNED A MEDAL

The line-ups and Gedenktafel are in the football club's 25-year history. Information about Alfred Lippold is

ACKNOWLEDGEMENTS

in lists of soldiers who were awarded medals, in Sächsisches Staatsarchiv. The activities of IR133 are described in Johannes Niemann's book *Das 9. Königlich Sächsische Infanterie-Regiment Nr. 133 Im Weltkrieg 1914–18* (1969). Albert Schmidt's grave is registered at Volksbund Deutsche Kriegsgräberfürsorge.

FROM AFRICA TO GLASGOW
I have read in the official battalion history *An Reisimeid Chataich – The 93rd Sutherland Highlanders* (1928) and the pamphlet *The 2nd Battalion Argyll & Sutherland Highlanders, 1914–1918*. The Regimental magazine *A Thin Red Line* has some information about football. The local newspapers are in Airdrie Library. Scottish Football Historical Archive has results of 93rd's matches.

A SHORT MARCH TO THE TRAIN
Johannes Niemann wrote the war history of the IR133. He also appeared in the BBC film 'Christmas Day Passed Quietly', broadcast at Christmas 1968, held by the IWM. There are other accounts of the regiment's war in *Unser Vormarsch bis zur Marne* (1915), by an anonymous Saxon officer and in *Aus der Geschichte des früheren kgl. Sächs. 9. Infanterie-Regiments Nr 133* (1924), written by IR133's commander Franz von Kotsch. *The German Army in World War I* (1) by Nigel Thomas (2003) has information about the Saxon army. *Dienstunterricht des Königlich Sächsischen Infanteristen* (1914/15) describes the German system of conscription and also contains the articles of war. Information about how the German army grew after mobilization comes from *The World War One Source Book* by Philip J. Haythornthwaite (1992). Information about railway traffic is in *History of the First World War* by B.H. Liddell Hart (1972) and in *The First World War – To Arms* by Hew Strachan (2001). The number of German soldiers on the Western Front is given in the first two volumes of the official British history of the war, *Military Operations* (1925 and 1927), by J. E. Edmonds.

FIRST OVER THE CHANNEL
The second battalion of the regiment Royal Welch Fusiliers was also first over the Channel, but landed in Rouen on 11 August, according to J.C. Dunn in *The War the Infantry Knew* (1994). This battalion then joined the 93rd in the 19th Brigade. The first entry of the 93rd's war diary is dated 5 August. Much of the information in my story comes from the war diary. It is held in the National Archives in London and available on the Internet. Lyn Macdonald has described the War book in her book

1914 (1989). Henry Hyslop, an officer in the 93rd, wrote the most detailed diary in the battalion during the war. It is held in the regimental museum. A sound interview with Charles Ditcham is in the Imperial War Museum (IWM). James Cunningham, another officer has described the kilts in an account that is held by the regimental museum. The museum also holds Adam McLachlan's account. Some information about equipment comes from Wikipedia. The picture of soldiers in the Royal Welch Fusiliers who served during the whole war is in Dunn's book.

MARCHING ON
The title of E. Alexander Powell's book is *Fighting in Flanders* (1914).

GRAVES AT THE ROADSIDE
I have taken information about IR133 and the other Saxon regiment from Niemann's and the anonymous officer's books. Information about the German army comes from Hew Strachan's book. I have read several descriptions of the German war plan, one of them in John Keegan's *The First World War* (1999). The account of how German soldiers treated civilians in Belgium and France is in *German Atrocities 1914 – A History of Denial* by John Horne and Alan Kramer (2001). Frank Collier's account of the war is in the regimental museum.

THE FIRST DAY OF THE WAR
Most information about the 93rd in this and the following chapters come from Hyslop, from the battalion war diary and the official history of the war. I have used figures for the strengths of the armies given in Haythornthwaite's book. The German company commander was Walther Bloem, who wrote the book *Vormarsch* (1916).

A HALF BATTALION
Horace Smith-Dorrien's answer about the 93rd is in Macdonald's book. She also writes about Smith-Dorrien's telephone conversation with the British headquarters. James Jack's extensive diary is in *General Jack's Diary,* compiled by John Terraine (2000). The name of Arthur Conan Doyle's book is *The British Campaign in France and Flanders, Volume I – 1914* (1916).

TOWARDS PARIS
Information about the IR133 comes from Niemann's and von Kotsch's books. Helmuth von Moltke's quotes are in *Der erste Weltkrieg – Dokumente*, compiled by Helmut Otto and Karl Schmiedel (1983). The quote about sweat and blood is from Walther Bloem's book.

The German account of the beginning of war is in *Der Vormarsch der 3. Armee 1914*, a pamphlet written by an officer, Hauptmann Munzinger, who was also editor of the army's official newspaper.

A RETREAT THEY COULD NOT UNDERSTAND

I think John Keegan has written the clearest account of the battle of the Marne.

TURNING AROUND

The title of the book about Aidan Liddell is *With a Smile and a Wave*, by Peter Daybell (2005). It also has quotes from another officer, Graham Hutchison. The 93rd's battalion doctor was Frederick Chandler. Extracts from his letters and diary are in the book *A Doctor's War*, compiled by Geoffrey Chandler (2009).

BARBED WIRE

The number of soldiers in the 93rd is given by Jack. Information about artillery comes from *The Last Full Measure* by Michael Stephenson (2013) and *Tommy* by Richard Holmes (2004) and also from the Army museum in Stockholm and the Artillery museum in Kristianstad, Sweden. Macdonald has described how Horace Smith-Dorrien recognized the French howitzers by their sound. The British gunner was P.J. Campbell and he is quoted by Stephenson.

"RATHER A FORLORN HOPE"

John French's complaints about the new soldiers are described in the official British history of the war. It was the 11th Brigade that ordered the attack at Ploegsteert Wood. Its message to the 93rd after the attack is in the war diary.

A QUIET CHRISTMAS

Malcolm Brown and Shirley Seaton have written the most detailed account of the truce in *Christmas Truce* (1999). Oswald Tilley wrote the "Just you think..." letter. It is in the IWM. The museum of the Gordon Highlanders in Aberdeen has given me information about the truce. E.R.P. Berryman's letter is in the IWM. Kurt Zehmisch's diary is in In Flanders Fields museum in Ypres. Robert Grave's story 'Christmas Truce' is in *Complete Short Stories* (2008). The story about the beer barrels is in the war diary of the second battalion of the Royal Welch Fusiliers. The article 'Last Day of Chivalry' is from *The Kiwanis Magazine*, December 1964 – January 1965. It is in the IWM.

DELICIOUS SILENCE

The name of the 93rd's regimental magazine (the magazine of the battalion) is *The Thin Red Line*. It is in the regimental museum in Stirling.

NOBODY'S HOME GROUND

This is where I have seen information about German and British soldiers playing football or kicking a ball together: Niemann's book, Niemann in the BBC film, Glasgow News 2 January 1915 (The sergeant's letter, in Mitchell Library, Glasgow), Brown's and Seaton's book, Kurt Zehmisch's diary, Stanley Weintraub's book *Silent Night* (2002), *The First World War* by A.J.P. Taylor (1966), *Not a Shot Was Fired – Letters from the Christmas Truce of 1914* (Internet), *Maxtone Graham, Christmas Truce 1914 – Operation Plum Puddings* (Internet), *Mail online* (Internet), *Meetings in No Man's Land* (2007), in the section written by Malcolm Brown, National Army Museum, BBC and finally in a letter from Anna Lisa Berkling in 1977. She wrote to the Swedish radio programme "Svar i dag" (Today's answers) about the book *The Campaign of 1914 in France and Belgium* by G.H. Perris. Her father Per Albin Hansson, who was Sweden's Prime Minister, bought the book in London in 1915.

The quote from Douglas Haig is in the book about James Jack. Brown and Seaton describe the match, among other things Ian Stewart's meeting in No Man's Land, when he was given the picture of the IR133's team. The soldier who talked about ten thousand footballs was William Dawkins of the East Kents regiment. He is quoted by Weintraub. The soldier who said that it would have been impossible to play on the churned up ground was Gordon Runcie of the 6th battalion in the regiment Gordon Highlanders, quoted by Brown and Seaton.

A NEW TRUCE IN THE MUD
Aidan Liddell described how soldiers dug a new trench in an old latrine.

THERE WAS MORE TO THE CHRISTMAS TRUCE THAN...
Murdoch McKenzie Wood made his speech in Parliament on 31 March 1930. It is on the Internet. The Gordon Highlanders' museum gave me information about him. Bruce Bairnsfathers quote is in *Legends & Traditions of the Great War* (internet). Stanley Weintraub's quote is in his book. Niall Ferguson's analysis of Germany's war aims is in his book *The Pity of War* (1999).

I have also consulted *1914* by Malcolm Brown (2005), and *The Times History of the War,* published continuously during the war. Contributors to *The Long, Long Trail* and *Great War Forum* on the Internet have helped me. I have used *Wikipedia* and *Google Maps*.

People in the war

ALBERT SCHMIDT
Lance Corporal and football player from Schedewitz in Saxony.
His regiment was Das 9. Königlich Sächsische Infanterie-Regiment Nr. 133 (IR133 for short). The regiment belonged to the German Third Army, which was a Saxon army.

JAMES COYLE
Sergeant and football player from Edinburgh in Scotland.
He served in the 2nd Battalion of the regiment Argyll and Sutherland Highlanders. The battalion was usually called the 93rd, which was its former regimental number. It belonged to the 19th Brigade, which was not attached to a higher formation but was moved around when needed.

ESSLEMONT ADAMS, chaplain of the 6th Battalion of the Gordon Highlanders Regiment. He took the initiative to hold a shared funeral for British and German soldiers.

BRUCE BAIRNSFATHER, British officer and cartoonist.

E.R.P BERRYMAN, officer in the Indian regiment, the Garhwal Rifles, which belonged to the British Expeditionary Force (BEF). He described the Christmas Truce with a drawing.

FREDERICK CHANDLER, the 93rd's battalion doctor. He wrote a diary and letters and took photographs during the war.

FRANK COLLIER, soldier in the 93rd. He wrote an account of his time in the war.

JAMES CUNNINGHAM, officer in the 93rd. He wrote an account of his time in the war.

CHARLES DITCHAM, drummer in the 93rd. When the war broke out he was not yet a regular soldier and was not allowed to carry arms. There is a sound recording of an interview with him in the Imperial War Museum.

JOHN FRENCH, supreme commander of the BEF.

DOUGLAS HAIG, commander of the British First Army in 1915.

GRAHAM HUTCHISON, officer in the 93rd. He has written about his time in the war.

HENRY HYSLOP, officer in the 93rd. He was company commander, briefly battalion commander and then second in command. He wrote a detailed diary during the war.

JAMES JACK, officer in the staff of the 19th Brigade. At Christmas 1914 he commanded a company in the First Battalion of the Scottish Rifles Regiment, also called the Cameronians. This battalion belonged, together with the 93rd, to the 19th Brigade.

HUGO KLEMM, officer in the IR133. He told about football during the Christmas Truce.

FRANZ VON KOTSCH, commander of the IR133 at the beginning of the war. He wrote about the regiment.

AIDAN LIDDELL, officer in the 93rd. He led the machine gun section. He wrote a diary and letters and took photographs.

ALFRED LIPPOLD, soldier in the IR133 and football player from Schedewitz.

ADAM MCLACHLAN, soldier in the 93rd. He wrote an account of his time in the war.

HELMUT VON MOLTKE, supreme commander of the German armed forces.

JOHANNES NIEMANN, officer in the IR133. He wrote the regiment's war history and also told about the Christmas Truce in a BBC film in 1968.

HENRY RAWLINSON, British general.

HORACE SMITH-DORRIEN, commander of the British Second Army Corps, where the 93rd and the other battalions in the 19th Brigade belonged during the battle of Le Cateau on 26 August.

J STEVENSON, soldier in the 93rd. He wrote a brief diary.

IAN STEWART, officer in the 93rd. He went out into No Man's Land to meet the Germans on Christmas Eve.

KURT ZEHMISCH, German officer who wrote a detailed diary.